W9-AQG-547

Miss Kay's Duck Commander Kitchen:
641.597 Rob   158215

Wilton Public Library

DATE DUE			

Wilton Public Library
1215 Cypress Street
P.O. Box 447
Wilton, IA   52778

MISS KAY'S

DUCK COMMANDER

KITCHEN

FAITH, FAMILY, AND FOOD—
BRINGING OUR HOME
TO YOUR TABLE

KAY ROBERTSON
with CHRYS HOWARD

HOWARD BOOKS
A DIVISION OF SIMON & SCHUSTER, INC.
New York · Nashville · London · Toronto · Sydney · New Delhi

Wilton Public Library
PO Box 447
Wilton, IA 52778

Howard Books
A Division of Simon & Schuster, Inc.
1230 Avenue the Americas
New York, NY 10020

Copyright © 2013 by Kay Robertson

All rights reserved, including the right to reproduce this book or portions thereof
in any form whatsoever. For information address Howard Books Subsidiary
Rights Department, 1230 Avenue the Americas, New York, NY 10020.

First Howard Books hardcover edition November 2013

HOWARD and colophon are trademarks of Simon & Schuster, Inc.

For information about special discounts for bulk purchases, please contact Simon & Schuster
Special Sales at 1-866-506-1949 or business@simonandschuster.com.

The Simon & Schuster Speakers Bureau can bring authors to your live event.
For more information or to book an event, contact the Simon & Schuster Speakers Bureau
at 1-866-248-3049 or visit our website at www.simonspeakers.com.

Scripture marked NIV taken from THE HOLY BIBLE, NEW INTERNATIONAL VERSION®, NIV®.
Copyright © 1973, 1978, 1984, 2011 by Biblica, Inc.® Used by Permission Biblica, Inc.®
All rights reserved worldwide.

Scripture taken from *The Message*. Copyright © 1993, 1994, 1995, 1996, 2000, 2001, 2002.
Used by permission of NavPress Publishing Group.

Permissions acknowledgments for photographs appear on page 237.

Designed by Timothy Shaner, nightanddaydesign.biz

Manufactured in the United States of America

1 3 5 7 9 10 8 6 4 2

Library of Congress Cataloging-in-Publication Data

Robertson, Kay, 1946–
    Miss Kay's Duck Commander kitchen : faith, family, and food—
bringing our home to your table / Kay Robertson with Chrys Howard.
        p.—cm.
    1. Cooking, American—Louisiana style. 2. Duck dynasty (Television
program). I. Howard, Chrys, 1953– II. Title.
    TX715.2.L68R66 2013
    641.59763—dc23
                                                    2013020326

ISBN 978-1-4767-6320-0   ISBN 978-1-4767-4512-1 (pbk)   ISBN 978-1-4767-4513-8 (ebook)

Every time I think of you—and I think of you often!—I thank God for your lives of free and open access to God, given by Jesus. There's no end to what has happened in you—it's beyond speech, beyond knowledge. The evidence of Christ has been clearly verified in your lives.

—1 Corinthians 1:4–6, *The Message*

Dedication

I always prayed for my boys to choose girls who would help them get to heaven and have the same lasting love as their dad and me. I will say that they chose wisely. I dedicate this book to my sweet daughters-in-law, who love, honor, and respect my boys.

To Lisa—thank you for your servant heart. You work harder than anyone I know, and no job is beneath you. I love how you adore Alan and treat Phil and me with such respect. Your example of standing strong and being willing to do the hard things in order to grow in the Lord makes us all better people.

To Missy—I knew Jase was looking for a mate who loved the Lord more than anything. Thank you for being exactly who Jase needs, for literally putting a song in my heart with your beautiful voice, and for sharing Jase's goal of getting your children, first, and then the rest of the world to heaven.

To Korie—Willie never did lack attention from the girls, but a very special girl got his heart for life. Your warm, loving nature makes you a joy to be around. You never act ugly and always treat others with love and respect. Thank you for holding Willie up, for standing beside him in business, and for being the kind of mom every kid dreams of having.

To Jessica—the one who stole the heart of my youngest son, thank you for keeping us all young. Your energetic spirit and love for people challenges us to live life with joy and confidence. You adore Jep as much as I do, and I love you for that.

Thank you all for the gift of your friendship, which no amount of money will buy! I love you all.

Pray for us. We have no doubts about what we're doing or why, but it's hard going and we need your prayers. All we care about is living well before God.

—Hebrews 13:20–22, *The Message*

Contents

Dear Friends

Well, dreams do come true! I've always wanted to write a cookbook and open a restaurant. Now one of those dreams is coming true. I'm still waiting on the restaurant, but at my age, I'm good with just cooking for my family. I do want to thank you for buying my cookbook. It means so much to me.

I've always loved to cook. I learned while watching my grandmother cook and care for our family. As a child, shelling peas and husking corn were two of my favorite activities—mainly because those were the times when I got to sit and talk to my Nanny. My first memories of food were about getting closer to my family. I believe that's why I love cooking so much. Cooking is so much more than just putting food together in a way that people will eat it. We know from all the fast-food chains that people will pretty much eat anything prepared for them. But real cooking involves putting time and effort into food preparation for one reason only—because you love the ones you're going to sit down and eat with.

To this day, when my family comes to visit, it's likely they will all be in the kitchen surrounding me while I stir a pot or roll out a piecrust. There will be lots of conversation and plenty of laughter. Later we'll crowd around our kitchen table, say grace, and enjoy the food and fellowship. If your family has gotten away from this habit, I would encourage you to begin today to sit down together for a meal at some point in the day. I know you're all busy and may not be able to do this every day, but when you can, do it. Your family will be blessed by this simple action.

With this cookbook, I am not saying I am the greatest cook or the most experienced cook, but I am saying I'm a good cook with lots of experience in cooking for family. In this cookbook, you'll find recipes each of my family members love as well as some old favorites. I hope you enjoy reading it and cooking from it.

May God bless you and your family.

—Miss Kay

Cast-Iron Skillet

For most of my recipes, I use a cast-iron skillet or cast-iron Dutch oven. This is how I learned to cook, so of course I think it's the best. In our earliest colonial days, the cast-iron skillet was used because modern stoves hadn't been invented. Entire meals were cooked in cast-iron pots. The pots needed to be hung over a fire, so they had a handle, or just stood in the fire on legs. After modern stoves came into use, the legs came off and other types of handles were added. These days, cast iron can be bought preseasoned, which means it's ready for use. If a skillet isn't preseasoned, seasoning it is essential.

Seasoning is the process of treating the surface of a cast-iron skillet so your food won't stick and your skillet won't rust. Seasoning is done by applying a thin layer of oil and then heating the skillet. I'm going to quickly tell you how it's done. First, you should wash and thoroughly dry your pan. Then coat it inside and out with any cooking oil. Don't forget the lid and outside of the pot. Next, put the skillet in the oven and heat it at 300°F for about 30 minutes or at 200°F for 2 to 3 hours. Let it cool to room temperature while in the oven, then repeat the process three or four times. Your skillet will now be ready for all these delicious recipes. Be sure to thoroughly dry your skillet and spray it with cooking spray or oil after each use.

I love cast iron because it heats up quickly and distributes heat more evenly than other cookware materials. You can use it on top of the stove or in the oven. And it can be used for quick frying or slow cooking. At one point in American history, cast iron was considered part of a woman's dowry. Well, I didn't come with cast iron, but I sure learned how to use it and love it. I hope you do, too!

MISS KAY'S
DUCK COMMANDER
KITCHEN

1.

Cooking
for Phil

〜〜〜〜〜〜〜〜〜〜〜〜〜〜〜〜〜〜〜

We got married in a fever,

hotter than a pepper sprout.

—June Carter Cash

Husbands, go all out in your love for your wives, exactly as Christ did for the church—a love marked by giving, not getting. Christ's love makes the church whole. His words evoke her beauty. Everything he does and says is designed to bring the best out of her, dressing her in dazzling white silk, radiant with holiness. And that is how husbands ought to love their wives. They're really doing themselves a favor—since they're already "one" in marriage.

—Ephesians 5:28, *The Message*

Turnip Greens, Fried Chicken, & Gravy

One day, when we were first married, I had gotten a mess of turnip greens and really didn't know what to do with them. I did figure they had to be washed, so I rinsed them off and threw them in a pot to boil. Later that night Phil came in the kitchen, took the lid off the greens, and chomped down a big bite. His face looked a little odd. Then he said, "Did you add sugar to the greens?" I said no.

He looked down in the pot, then looked at me with another odd look and said, "How many times did you rinse them?" I said, "Once." He calmly put the lid back on the greens and just said, "Dirt." I didn't know that turnips greens had to be washed over and over again to get the dirt out. Apparently Phil did.

Another time I was so excited to cook some chicken and gravy for my hungry man. In those days, you didn't buy chickens all cut up in nice pieces; you had to do that yourself. No one had ever given me a cutting lesson, so I got that whole chicken and cut and cut. Phil said it was so hacked up he didn't know what part was what. That might not have been so bad if it wasn't for the gravy that was intended to cover it up. Somehow I got the amounts mixed up and added more flour and less water than was supposed to be mixed together. That gravy looked more like

Above: We've come a long way in our forty-plus years of marriage. This picture was taken in 1969, when Phil had just graduated from college.

brown custard than it did gravy.

These stories are two of the many that we have laughed at when we remember our early years of marriage. Neither one of us was perfect then, nor are we now. Many times young people get confused, thinking they can find the "perfect" mate. I want you to know that "perfect" people don't exist. I married Phil when I was sixteen, which was young to marry even for the 1960s, when the average marrying age was around twenty. Marrying that young is not something I would ever recommend, but I do know this: marriage isn't about finding the perfect person and then settling down for the perfect life. It's about living up to a commitment you made and learning to love the person you are committed to.

Trust me, we have been through some hard times, worse times than bad gravy on chopped-up chicken and dirty turnip greens. But we stuck together and are so proud of the family we have now. We have four incredible sons, four loving daughters-in-law, fourteen God-honoring grandchildren, and two beautiful great-granddaughters—all because we chose to stay together and love each other. 🦆

Above: We love getting our big family together. Just after we took this photo, the kids ran to the swings and the adults sat around and talked. Even a photo shoot can be fun! **Opposite:** *Here we are celebrating the fortieth anniversary of Duck Commander. I had always dreamed of marrying a "pioneer" man who could live off the land. Phil dreamed of inventing a duck call that really sounded like a duck. With the help of our good Lord, both our dreams have come true.*

Pork & Chicken Chow Mein

Makes 6 to 8 servings • Large skillet with a lid

¼ cup vegetable oil

4 boneless pork chops (about 1 pound), cut in small pieces

1 bi-pack can (42 ounces) chicken chow mein dinner

1 can (28 ounces) chop suey vegetables

3 tablespoons soy sauce

3 tablespoons teriyaki marinade and sauce

Just Right White Rice (page 110), for serving

1. Heat the oil in a large skillet over medium heat and brown the pork pieces.

2. Stir in the chow mein, vegetables, soy sauce, and teriyaki marinade. Put the lid on and simmer for 10 to 15 minutes, until the pork is cooked through and the vegetables are hot.

3. Serve over rice.

A Note from Miss Kay

I know what you're thinking—surely Phil doesn't eat chow mein? *Yep, he does. In fact he even eats sushi now! One of our grocery stores makes sushi, and Phil has me stop often and bring him some. Hey—good food is good food from any country!*

Pecan Pie

Makes 1 (9-inch) pie • Electric mixer

3 large eggs

¾ cup sugar

½ stick (4 tablespoons) butter, softened

½ teaspoon salt

1 teaspoon vanilla extract

½ cup light corn syrup (I use Karo)

½ cup maple syrup (I use Johnnie Fair) or honey

1½ cups pecan halves

1 (9-inch) piecrust, homemade (page 182) or store-bought, unbaked

1. Heat the oven to 350°F.

2. Beat the eggs with the mixer until fluffy, about 8 minutes.

3. In another mixing bowl, stir together the sugar, butter, salt, vanilla, and syrups. Gently fold this into the eggs. Gently fold in the pecans. Pour the filling into the piecrust.

4. Bake for 40 to 50 minutes, until the filling is set and no longer wobbly in the center.

5. Let cool completely before cutting.

A Note from Miss Kay

This is Phil's favorite, and the good news is he makes it himself! I make the crust while he is mixing together the pie filling, and in no time we have a fresh pie on the counter. Everyone declares it's the best they've ever tasted.

Chocolate Pie

Makes 2 (9-inch) pies • Double boiler • Electric mixer

Pie Filling

1 stick (¼ pound) butter

5 squares (5 ounces) unsweetened chocolate (I use Baker's), chopped

2 cups sugar

⅔ cup all-purpose flour

1 teaspoon salt

1 can (12 ounces) evaporated milk (I use Pet)

1 cup whole milk

6 large egg yolks, lightly beaten (save the whites for the meringue)

1 teaspoon vanilla extract

2 (9-inch) piecrusts, homemade (page 182) or store-bought, baked as directed

Meringue

6 large egg whites

1 cup sugar

1 to 1½ teaspoons vanilla extract

1. Make the pie filling: In the top of a double boiler over simmering water, melt the butter and chocolate. Beat in the sugar, flour, and salt. Add both milks and stir continuously until the mixture thickens. This may take up to 30 minutes.

2. Once it's thickened, stir a little into the egg yolks. This will temper the yolks and keep them from cooking too fast. Stir the tempered egg yolks into the mixture in the double boiler and cook, stirring, for 1 minute.

3. Remove the top from the double boiler. Stir the vanilla into the filling and set aside to cool.

4. Pour the filling into the piecrusts.

5. Make the meringue: Heat the broiler. With the mixer, beat the egg whites on high speed for 3 to 4 minutes, until soft peaks form. Gradually beat in the sugar, then beat in the vanilla. (By now, the peaks should be able to stand and bend over as you remove the beaters.) Spread the meringue over the pie filling.

6. Put the pies under the broiler to brown the meringue. (Watch carefully, as this will only take about 30 seconds.)

7. Chill the pies thoroughly before serving.

A Note from Miss Kay

Meringue can be scary to make, but you can do it. With a little practice you will be impressing your family with a perfect chocolate pie!

Swiss Steak & Sautéed Mushrooms

Makes 4 to 8 servings • Dutch oven or flameproof casserole dish with a lid • Large cast-iron skillet

1 package (about 1 pound) tenderized round steak (see Tip)

Salt and black pepper

3 tablespoons all-purpose flour

Vegetable oil

2 celery stalks, chopped in large chunks

1 onion, chopped in large chunks

1 garlic clove, chopped

1 bell pepper, chopped in large chunks

1 can (14.5 ounces) diced tomatoes

1 can (8 ounces) tomato sauce

Sautéed Mushrooms (recipe follows), for serving

1. Heat the oven to 275°F.

2. Season the meat with salt and pepper. Sprinkle the steaks lightly with flour on both sides.

3. Heat a small amount of oil in the Dutch oven and brown the steaks on both sides. Drain off extra oil, keeping the browned drippings in the pan. Add the celery, onion, garlic, bell pepper, tomatoes, and tomato sauce. Cover and bake for 1½ hours.

4. Serve with the sautéed mushrooms on the side.

Tip Tenderized round steaks usually come 4 to a package. Cut in half so you have 8 pieces.

Sautéed Mushrooms

1 stick (¼ pound) butter

1 onion, chopped

Dash of liquid smoke (see Tip)

Dash of teriyaki sauce

Dash of soy sauce

Dash of Worcestershire sauce

¼ cup red wine

1 pound mushrooms, sliced or left whole if small

Duck Commander Cajun Seasoning (mild or zesty)

1. Melt the butter in the skillet over medium-low heat. Add the onion and cook, stirring occasionally, until tender, about 8 minutes.

2. Add the liquid smoke, teriyaki, soy, and Worcestershire sauces, the red wine, mushrooms, and Cajun seasoning to taste and bring to a simmer. Simmer until the liquid reduces some and the mushrooms are tender.

Tip A dash would be to just turn the bottle over and shake it one or two times.

A Note from Miss Kay

Sautéed mushrooms are a simple recipe but really add to a meal like Swiss steak and potatoes. Remember that mushrooms can lose some flavor if soaked and washed, so just wipe them off with a damp paper towel.

Egg Custard Pie

Makes 2 (9-inch) pies

½ stick (4 tablespoons) butter, softened

¾ cup sugar

Pinch of salt

4 large eggs

1 can (14 ounces) sweetened condensed milk (I use Eagle Brand)

2 cups whole milk, warmed

½ teaspoon vanilla extract

2 (9-inch) piecrusts, homemade (page 182) or store-bought, baked as directed

1. Heat the oven to 425°F.

2. In a mixing bowl, beat the butter, sugar, and salt until creamy. Add the eggs one at a time, beating after each egg is added. Add the condensed milk, whole milk, and vanilla and mix thoroughly. Pour into the piecrusts.

3. Bake for 10 minutes. Reduce the oven heat to 300°F and bake 25 minutes more, until the filling is set and no longer wobbly in the center.

A Note from Miss Kay

Many young folks don't think they like egg custard, but it's a delicious pie. Give it a try. You can also top it with berries of your choice.

Red & Green Fruit Salad

Makes 4 servings

4 apples, 2 red and 2 green, cut into
½-inch chunks with skin on

2 celery stalks, chopped

1 cup coarsely chopped walnuts

¾ cup mayonnaise or salad dressing

Mix all the ingredients together in a large mixing bowl. Enjoy!

Korie is busy at work in Kay's kitchen.

A Note from Miss Kay

This is a simple variation of the Waldorf salad, and I call it our Red and Green Fruit Salad. It's perfect for Christmas with all its red and green colors. But you can make it any time of the year. You will love it!

Fried Round Steak & White Sauce

Makes 4 servings steak and about 1 cup sauce • Large cast-iron skillet • Medium saucepan

4 round or cubed steaks (about 1 pound, or enough for your family)
Salt and black pepper
¼ cup all-purpose flour
½ cup cooking oil

White Sauce

3 tablespoons butter
½ teaspoon salt
½ teaspoon black (or white) pepper
3 tablespoons all-purpose flour
1 cup milk

1. Season the meat with salt and pepper. Roll the steaks lightly in the flour on both sides.

2. Heat the oil in the skillet over medium heat. Cook the steaks in the oil on both sides until completely done, about 1 minute each side. Use a fork to test. (The juice should be clear.)

3. Drain on paper towels.

4. Make the white sauce: Melt the butter in the saucepan over medium heat. In a small bowl, mix the salt, pepper, and flour together. Add to the butter and stir until smooth. Add the milk slowly, stirring constantly until the sauce is hot and thickened.

5. Serve on top of the steaks.

A Note from Miss Kay

This is an old recipe, but still one of Phil's favorites. The white sauce is easy to double or triple, according to how many will be at your table tonight.

Pinto Beans & Sausage

Makes 6 to 8 servings • Slow cooker • Medium skillet • Small casserole dish • Large (7- to 8-quart) cooking pot

1 package (1 pound) pinto beans

1 package (2.4 ounces) Zatarain's Red Bean Seasoning

1 stick (¼ pound) butter

2 tablespoons olive oil

1 onion, finely chopped

2 tablespoons crushed garlic

1 hambone

1 package (1 pound) andouille sausage (we use hot sausage from Savoie's, but mild is good, too)

Just Right White Rice (page 110), for serving

Mexican Cornbread (page 55), for serving

1. Wash and rinse the beans in a strainer. Put in the slow cooker and fill with water ¾ of the way to the top. Cook on low overnight.

2. Drain off the water and rinse the beans again the next morning. (This reduces the gases in the beans.) Fill the cooker with fresh water ¾ of the way to the top again and add the seasoning.

3. In the skillet, melt the butter with the oil, then add the onion and garlic. Cook, stirring occasionally, until the vegetables are translucent, about 7 minutes. Add the vegetables to the beans. Cut off any meat from the hambone and add it to the beans. Stir it all together, then put the hambone in the cooker. Cook the beans on high for 4 hours.

4. While the beans are cooking, heat the oven to 250°F. Cut the sausage into small pieces and brown in the casserole in the oven for 20 minutes. Put them on a paper towel to drain off the grease.

5. When the beans are tender, pour them into the large pot and transfer to the stovetop. Add the sausage and cook on medium heat for 45 minutes to 1 hour.

6. Serve with rice and Mexican Cornbread. Yummy!

Note from Miss Kay

Pinto Beans and Sausage is the perfect meal to put on first thing in the morning and then head to work or run your errands. This is important for me, since we live several miles from town. Plus, when you get home, your house will smell so good!

Cheesy Corn Casserole

Makes 8 to 10 servings • 9 x 13-inch casserole dish

1 stick (¼ pound) butter, melted, plus a little more for the casserole

1 can (15.25 ounces) whole kernel corn, drained

1 can (14.75 ounces) cream-style corn

1 carton (8 ounces) sour cream

1 box (8.5 ounces) Jiffy corn muffin mix

2 cups grated cheese, divided: 1½ cups in mix and ½ cup sprinkled on top

1. Heat the oven to 375°F. Lightly butter the casserole dish.

2. Mix all the ingredients in a large bowl. Pour into the casserole dish. Bake for 45 minutes. Let cool a little before serving.

A Note from Miss Kay

As you would guess, we do eat our share of meat and seafood dishes, but we also like vegetables. Phil grew up with a family garden, so we love to get fresh vegetables as often as possible. This dish isn't made with fresh corn, but it's a great one for the winter months, when fresh corn isn't always available.

Phil's Famous Pralines

Makes about 12 pralines (repeat for more) • Heavy-bottomed medium saucepan • Wax paper

1 cup packed light brown sugar

1 cup granulated sugar

½ cup evaporated milk (I use Pet)

Pinch of salt

½ stick (4 tablespoons) butter, softened

1 teaspoon vanilla extract

1¼ cups coarsely chopped pecans

1. In the saucepan, bring the sugars, milk, and salt to a rolling boil, stirring occasionally.

2. When rolling boil starts, begin timing and cook for 4 minutes. (Accuracy is important.) While it's boiling, lay out wax paper on your counter.

3. Remove from the heat and add the butter, vanilla, and pecans. Beat vigorously until the mixture becomes thick. (Seriously, I do mean *vigorously*.)

4. Quickly drop by spoonfuls onto the wax paper. (Work quickly, otherwise it will harden too much to spoon out.) Let the pralines cool and set.

A Note from Miss Kay

This is another recipe that Phil takes responsibility for making. It's a candy, so precision is important. He's more patient than I am when it comes to candy-making projects. When you read the history of pralines, you find that early French settlers made them with almonds, but almonds were in short supply in Louisiana, so they turned to a more abundant nut, the pecan. In any case, we sure are glad they found their way into Louisiana cuisine!

2.

Feeding My Boys

∿∿∿∿∿∿∿∿∿∿∿∿∿∿∿∿∿∿∿∿

There is no sight on earth more appealing than the sight of a woman making dinner for someone she loves.

—Thomas Wolfe

Don't burn out; keep yourselves fueled and aflame. Be alert servants of the Master, cheerfully expectant. Don't quit in hard times; pray all the harder. Help needy Christians; be inventive in hospitality.

—Romans 12:13, *The Message*

Recipes My Boys Love

Every Man for Himself

I've worked hard to teach my boys good manners, but trust me, four hungry boys are never in the mood for a manners lesson. I have a couple of stories that may not speak of the most shining moments in my sons' lives, but they center around food, so I have to tell them.

Alan was six or seven years old and times were tough around our house, but we always had plenty of food. At least I thought we did. One day I was cleaning Alan's room and noticed a plate of food up in the closet. Naturally I questioned him about it. He said he couldn't eat it all at supper and he didn't want his little brother to get it, so he hid it. Logical, I guess. Little did I know that this "every man for himself" attitude would prevail with my boys—even today they are "lovingly" competitive in everything they do. You may have caught a glimpse of this while watching *Duck Dynasty*.

Here's another story that's even worse. We retell this story at least once a year around our house. It definitely shows both the competitive spirit and the love for food my boys have. Jase and Willie almost had a war over toast and frozen pizza. It seems Jase had buttered twelve slices of bread for toast and Willie had placed a frozen pizza (yes,

*Opposite: Who would have thought these four boys were destined for TV stardom? Certainly not me. Alan is the oldest. Then there's Jase on the left and Willie beside him and our baby, Jep. **Above:** Willie and Jase at the warehouse. I'm not sure what they're up to, but it's surely something crazy.*

moms, even I had frozen pizza in the freezer) on a pan ready to shove it in the oven. Well, we had only one oven. Jase needed to broil; Willie needed to bake. There seemed no solution except to fight it out, which they proceeded to do. I was not home at the time, or I would have put a stop to it immediately. But a friend of the boys named Don "Curly" Foster was there. The story goes that the only way he got them to stop fighting was to tell them they weren't acting like Christians. I'm not proud that they were fighting over toast and a frozen pizza, but I am proud that they recognized ungodly behavior. Thanks, Curly, for pointing them in the right direction that day.

Wow, do I love my boys, but they can be aggravating! We all have those great moments when we think our children are God's gift to the entire world, but we also have those moments when we want to hang a sign on our door that reads, "(Fill in the blank)'s mom does not live here!" Sometimes we literally might want to hide in the closet, like Alan's leftover supper.

As adult sons, these four boys tease and harass me to no end, but I love every minute of it. No, they're not perfect sons, and I know they still have some growing in the Lord to do, but I have confidence that God is doing a good work in them. I'm just grateful to be a part of the journey. 🐦

Above: I love this picture taken at the fortieth anniversary of Duck Commander. It was such a fun night. There were many old friends there to celebrate with us.

Jep's Best Baked Beans

Makes 8 servings • Microwave • 9x13-inch casserole dish

2 cans (28 ounces each) pork and beans (I use Van Camp's)

1 Vidalia onion, finely chopped

½ cup packed brown sugar (either light or dark is okay)

2 tablespoons yellow mustard

¾ cup BBQ sauce (I use Cattlemen's)

½ cup Johnnie Fair syrup (okay to use corn syrup)

6 slices bacon

1. Heat the oven to 400°F.

2. Mix together the beans, onion, sugar, mustard, BBQ sauce, and syrup and pour into the casserole.

3. Cook the bacon for 2 minutes in the microwave. Put on top of the beans.

4. Bake for 45 minutes to 1 hour, until bubbly and slightly thickened.

A Note from Miss Kay
This recipe makes repeated appearances in our family; it's a great one to serve with hamburgers.

Jase's Favorite Sweet Potato Pie

Makes 2 (9-inch) pies

3 cups mashed cooked sweet potatoes

2 cups sugar

6 large eggs

1½ teaspoons ground cinnamon

½ teaspoon grated nutmeg

½ teaspoon salt

1 stick (¼ pound) butter, softened

1 can (12 ounces) evaporated milk
    (I use Pet)

1½ teaspoons vanilla extract

2 (9-inch) piecrusts, homemade (page
    182) or store-bought, unbaked

1. Heat the oven to 350°F.

2. To get 3 cups mashed sweet potatoes, boil about 2¼ pounds whole sweet potatoes with the skin on for about 40 minutes, until they are soft. Drain, let cool until you can handle them, and remove the skin. Mash the potatoes in a large mixing bowl. Let them mostly cool.

3. Beat in the sugar, eggs, cinnamon, nutmeg, salt, butter, milk, and vanilla. Pour into the unbaked piecrusts.

4. Bake for 10 minutes, then reduce the oven heat to 300°F. Bake for 45 to 50 minutes more, until the filling is set and no longer wobbly in the center.

A Note from Miss Kay

At our house, this is one of Jase's favorites, so if you're not right by the oven when the pie comes out, watch out! It might disappear before you get a bite!

Jase's Favorite Creamed Potatoes

Makes 6 servings • Large saucepan • Electric mixer

Salt

4 large russet potatoes, peeled and cut into chunks

½ stick (4 tablespoons) butter, softened

Black pepper

½ to ¾ cup evaporated milk (I use Pet)

1. Fill the saucepan with salted water and bring to a boil. Place potato chunks in the boiling water and cook until tender.

2. Drain the potatoes in a colander and transfer to a large mixing bowl. Add the butter and season with salt and pepper. Beat with the mixer on medium-high speed and slowly add the milk. Mix until creamy smooth.

A Note from Miss Kay

Jase always lets me know if there are any lumps in my potatoes so, believe me, I work to keeps those lumps out. I guess my boys are spoiled by my cooking, but I do love to cook for them and anyone else.

Jase's Choice, Italian Crème Cake

Makes 1 (9-inch) cake • 3 (9-inch) round cake pans • Wire cooling racks • Electric mixer
Nonstick cooking spray and flour, for the pans

Cake Layers

2 cups sugar
1 stick (¼ pound) butter, softened
½ cup vegetable shortening (I use Crisco)
5 large eggs, separated
2 cups all-purpose flour
1 teaspoon baking soda
½ teaspoon salt
1 cup buttermilk
1 cup pecans, toasted and coarsely chopped
1 cup shredded coconut
1 teaspoon vanilla extract

Cream Cheese Frosting

1 stick (¼ pound) butter, softened
1 package (8 ounces) cream cheese, softened
1 teaspoon vanilla extract
1 package (1 pound) powdered sugar
½ cup chopped pecans

A Note from Miss Kay
This is another of Jase's favorite recipes. Italian Crème Cake takes a little longer to make than a cake from a mix, so it really says, "I love you."

1. Heat the oven to 350°F. Grease and flour the cake pans.

2. Make the cake layers: In a large mixing bowl, cream together the sugar, butter, and shortening. Add the egg yolks one at a time, mixing well.

3. Sift together the flour, baking soda, and salt. Add the flour mixture and the buttermilk to the batter in 3 batches, beginning and ending with flour. Mix well. Stir in the pecans, coconut, and vanilla.

4. In a separate bowl, beat the egg whites to stiff peaks with the mixer. (The peaks will stay standing when you remove the beaters.) Gently fold into the batter.

5. Pour the batter into the pans. Bake until the layers start to pull away at the sides and a toothpick inserted in the center of a layer comes out clean, about 25 minutes.

6. Let the layers cool in the pans for a few minutes, then run a spatula around the sides and invert the layers onto a wire rack to cool completely.

7. While the layers are cooling, make the frosting: Beat together the butter, cream cheese, vanilla, and sugar with the mixer until fluffy. (The frosting will appear stiff at first, but will soften as you mix it.)

8. When the cake layers are cool, frost the top of one layer. Put another layer on top and frost that layer. Put the last layer on top and frost the top and sprinkle with the pecans.

Willie's Favorite Roast with Vegetables

Makes 2 to 3 servings per pound of meat • Dutch oven or roasting pan

Cooking oil

Salt and black pepper

1 boneless chuck, sirloin tip, rib eye, or rump roast, 3 to 4 pounds

All-purpose flour

New or red potatoes (3 per person) or large white butter potatoes (1 per person)

Duck Commander Cajun Seasoning (mild or zesty) or other Cajun seasoning (optional)

1 pound carrots, peeled, ends cut off, cut in large chunks

1 medium onion, peeled and left whole

Fresh mushrooms, as many as you like (optional)

A Note from Miss Kay

There was a time when roast was the Sunday meal instead of something from the local restaurant. It was and still is something you can put in the oven when you leave for church and it will be perfect when you arrive home three hours later. The entire meal is in one pot—meat and vegetables. In our family, Phil makes a regular brown gravy with the drippings. Add a salad and rolls and you're done!

1. Heat the oven to 300°F.

2. Put about 1 inch of oil in the bottom of the Dutch oven. Turn the heat to medium.

3. Salt and pepper the roast, then coat it with flour. Put the roast in the pan; brown the outside, turning it to get all sides browned. Remove the roast from the pan, drain off the oil, and put the roast back in the pan.

4. If you're using large potatoes, peel and quarter them. You can leave small, fresh new potatoes whole. In a mixing bowl, roll the potatoes in a little oil to coat them. Add the seasoning (or just salt and pepper) to taste and make sure they're seasoned all over. Add the potatoes to the pan.

5. Add the carrots, onion, and mushrooms, if using. (The vegetables need to be chunky so they won't cook too quickly.)

6. Bake for 20 minutes per pound, usually 2½ to 3 hours, according to the size roast.

7. Remove from the oven and transfer the meat and vegetables to a platter. Use the drippings in the pan to make gravy.

Jep's Pick, Chicken Fajitas

Makes 8 to 10 fajitas • Deep skillet (cast-iron or regular) with a lid • Small skillet

1½ sticks (12 tablespoons) butter, plus more for the tortillas

½ bell pepper, chopped

½ white onion, chopped

4 to 6 skinless, boneless chicken breasts, cut into bite-size pieces

¼ cup Worcestershire sauce

1 tablespoon liquid smoke

1 teaspoon salt

Duck Commander Cajun Seasoning (mild or zesty)

8 to 10 flour tortillas (7-inch size)

Toppings: shredded cheese, lettuce, sour cream, salsa

1. Combine the butter, bell pepper, and onion in the skillet and cook on medium-high heat until the vegetables are softened.

2. Add the chicken, Worcestershire sauce, liquid smoke, salt, and Cajun seasoning to taste. Cover with a lid and cook, stirring occasionally, until all the liquid has cooked out of the pot and the chicken is cooked through.

3. While the chicken is cooking, melt a small amount of butter in the small skillet. Cook a single tortilla at a time on both sides on medium heat until it is browned. Repeat for all tortillas.

4. Fill the tortillas with the chicken-vegetable mix. Top with your desired toppings and serve.

A Note from Miss Kay

This is Missy's recipe, and everyone in the family loves it. I wanted to include it and this seemed like the best chapter for it since it's a favorite of Jep's. There are lots of variations to this recipe, so have fun with it.

Willie's Choice, Deviled Eggs

Makes 24 deviled eggs

12 large eggs
2 tablespoons sweet relish
1½ teaspoons dill pickle relish
1 teaspoon yellow mustard
About ¾ cup mayonnaise or salad
   dressing
Salt and black pepper
Paprika (optional)

1. Boil and peel eggs (see Tips). If the eggs aren't cold, chill them.

2. Cut the eggs in half lengthwise. Gently scoop out the yolks with a spoon and put them in a bowl. Add the relishes, mustard, mayonnaise, and salt and pepper. Mash all the ingredients together, then taste. Add more mustard, salt, and pepper if you think it's needed. More mayonnaise can be added if it seems dry.

3. Spoon back into the egg whites. Sprinkle with paprika, if desired.

Tips for Hard-Boiling & Peeling Eggs

Put the eggs in a saucepan that has a lid and cover with water. Set on the burner on high and bring the water to a boil. As soon as it reaches a rapid boil, remove the pot from the stove and cover it tightly. Set the timer for 17 minutes for large eggs or 20 minutes for extra-large eggs. When the timer goes off, drain the hot water.

   My peeling technique is to drain the hot water, crack the eggshells all over, then cover them with cold water or run cold water over them. This makes getting the shells off easier.

A Note from Miss Kay

Why do we all love deviled eggs? Because they are so good! Deviled eggs are a "try a little this and a little that" kind of recipe, so experiment for yourself. You can't go wrong. Whatever you do, I promise, they will disappear.

Wilton Public Library
PO Box 447
Wilton, IA 52778

Willie's Favorite Fried Chicken

Makes about 4 servings • Large deep cast-iron skillet with a lid
Deep-fry thermometer (if you fry a lot, you won't need this; you'll just know)

1 tablespoon Duck Commander Cajun
   Seasoning (mild or zesty)
2 teaspoons black pepper
1 teaspoon salt
1 teaspoon chili powder
1 teaspoon Old Bay Seasoning
1 chicken (3½ to 4½ pounds), cut up,
   or purchase just the parts your
   family eats
2 large eggs
2 cups buttermilk
½ teaspoon Tabasco sauce
Cooking oil, for frying
2 cups all-purpose flour

1. In a large bowl, mix together the Cajun
   seasoning, pepper, salt, chili powder, and Old Bay.
   Roll the chicken pieces in the seasoning mixture.
   If you need more seasoning, mix more.

2. In a large bowl, beat the eggs. Mix in the
   buttermilk and Tabasco. Add the chicken pieces
   and make sure they are all coated.

3. Fill the skillet about ½ full with oil. Turn on to
   medium-to-high heat.

4. One at a time, take the chicken pieces out of the
   bowl and roll them in the flour. Set aside.

5. When the oil is hot (350°F), carefully add the
   chicken pieces. Brown them on all sides.

6. Cover and cook for about 15 minutes more,
   turning as necessary, until cooked through. The
   chicken should turn a golden brown. Use a fork to
   test. (The juices should be clear.)

7. Drain on paper towels and serve.

A Note from Miss Kay
I know it's easier to pick up
chicken on the way home,
but it's never as good as
homemade fried chicken, or at least
that's what Willie says. He loves
homemade fried chicken, and really,
if you're in the kitchen anyway, it's
not that hard!

Jep's Meatloaf Choice

Makes 6 servings • 2 loaf pans (9 x 5 inches each)

3 pounds hamburger meat

2 celery stalks, finely chopped (about ⅔ cup)

1 medium onion, finely chopped (about ⅔ cup)

3 garlic cloves, finely chopped

1 small bell pepper, finely chopped (about ⅔ cup)

2 large eggs

1 tablespoon Duck Commander Cajun Seasoning (mild or zesty)

1 tablespoon black pepper

1 can (12 ounces) tomato paste

2 tablespoons evaporated milk

2 sleeves Ritz crackers, crushed

2 cans (8 ounces each) tomato sauce, for topping

4 slices bacon, cut in half crosswise

1. Heat the oven to 375°F.

2. In a large bowl, mix together (with your hands) the meat, celery, onion, garlic, bell pepper, eggs, Cajun seasoning, black pepper, tomato paste, milk, and 2 cups of the crushed crackers. Divide between 2 loaf pans. Spread tomato sauce on the top of each loaf. Sprinkle the remaining crushed crackers on top of the sauce. Top the loaves with the bacon.

3. Bake for 1 hour to 1 hour 10 minutes, until set and the juices run clear when the meatloaf is poked with a fork. Let cool a little before slicing.

A Note from Miss Kay

Meatloaf was a standard meal when we were growing up because it's economical yet still a great choice for dinner. Jep has always been my "meatloaf lover" and can't wait for me to make it. You can serve it with potatoes of any kind and a simple salad.

Alan's Favorite Coconut Cream Pie

Makes 2 (9-inch) pies • Double boiler • Electric mixer

Pie Filling

2 sticks (½ pound) butter
2 cups sugar
⅔ cup all-purpose flour
1 teaspoon salt
1 can (12 ounces) evaporated milk
    (I use Pet)
1 cup regular milk
6 large egg yolks, lightly beaten (save
    the whites for the meringue)
1 teaspoon vanilla extract
1 package (14 ounces) sweetened
    shredded coconut

2 (9-inch) piecrusts, homemade
    (page 182) or store-bought,
    baked as directed

Meringue

6 large egg whites
1 cup sugar
1 to 1½ teaspoons vanilla extract

1. Make the pie filling: In the top of a double boiler over simmering water, melt the butter. Beat in the sugar, flour, and salt. Add the milks and stir continuously until the mixture thickens. This may take up to 30 minutes.

2. Once it's thickened, stir a little into the egg yolks. This will temper the yolks and keep them from cooking too fast. Stir the tempered egg yolks into the mixture in the double boiler and cook, stirring, for 1 minute.

3. Remove the top from the double boiler. Stir the vanilla and all but 1 cup of the coconut into the filling. Pour the filling into the piecrusts.

4. Make the meringue: Heat the broiler. With the mixer, beat the egg whites on high speed for 3 to 4 minutes, until soft peaks form. Gradually beat in the sugar, then beat in the vanilla. (By now, the peaks should be able to stand and bend over as you remove the beaters.) Spread the meringue over the pie filling.

5. Put the pies under the broiler to brown the meringue. (Watch carefully, as this will only take about 30 seconds.) Sprinkle the reserved 1 cup of coconut on top. Chill the pies thoroughly before serving.

A Note from Alan

I have to admit that I have a sweet tooth, which means I'm constantly on a diet. But I can't resist Mom's coconut cream pie. It's so creamy and delicious. I know you'll love it, too.

3.

The Women My Boys Love Learn to Cook

~~~~~~

When baking, follow directions.

When cooking, go by your own taste.

—Laiko Bahrs

But Ruth said, "Don't force me to leave you; don't make me go home. Where you go, I go; and where you live, I'll live. Your people are my people, your God is my god; where you die, I'll die, and that's where I'll be buried, so help me GOD— not even death itself is going to come between us!"

—Ruth 1:16–17, *The Message*

Recipes from the Women My Boys Love

My Sons & Their Wives

Alan is our oldest son and was there during the roughest years of our marriage—our beginning years. He took on many responsibilities because I had to work and Phil wasn't living right. To this day, Alan leads our family in so many ways. He married Lisa when he was very young. They have had their ups and downs, but God has blessed their faithfulness to Him and today they have two married daughters and two granddaughters. Lisa is the one who volunteers for everything in our family. She travels with me and helps me look decent at my performances. She cooks when we have big family gatherings. Since Alan was a preacher for many years, Lisa has blessed many lives by sharing her life story with others. Lisa also tells others that God is bigger than any problem they may have. Lisa is like a big sister to my other daughters-in-law, the big sister everyone hopes to have.

Jase, our second son, always seemed to know his destiny was working in our family business. As a teen, he was a leader in our local youth group, where he met Missy. Once he and Missy started dating, they knew they were meant for each other and wedding bells rang pretty quickly. Missy has turned into a great cook and is always willing to open her home for showers and parties or to feed

Above: Alan and Lisa with me and the boys: Jase, Willie, cousin John Gimber, and Jep. I look like I was in shock. I'm not sure what that was about! (1984)

the youth group or her boy's football or baseball teams. A unique treat for our family is Missy's singing ability. We all love to sing, but Missy can *really* sing. We love it when she sings a solo at church or leads us in songs at home. What a blessing she is to the Robertson clan!

Willie is my third son and my most energetic one! He's always "got a project." From the time he sold candy at school to raise money to today as he leads our company, Willie has shown his talent for running a business. For a long time, Willie wasn't sure where he could make his mark in our company, since it was already up and running by the time he graduated from college, but he certainly figured it out! He met his sweet wife at Camp Ch-Yo-Ca, a Christian camp we all love, when Korie was just in the third grade. I think she won his heart with her gentle spirit. Korie probably cooks the least of my daughters-in-law, but Willie loves to cook so much, she doesn't have to. Anyway, she's pretty busy with her five kids and helping run our company, too. Korie's got a "business" head, and we all depend on her to help us make decisions. Any time I feel unsettled about something, I just call Korie. She is the calm in any storm.

Above: Jase and Missy were married at our church, White's Ferry Road Church of Christ. Look at that tux and tails on Jase! (1990) **Opposite above:** *Korie and Willie were also married at our church. It was the biggest wedding I had ever seen. At least Phil tucked his shirt in! (1992)* **Opposite:** *Jep and Jessica had a beautiful outside wedding at the house of our good friends Mary and Mac Owen, right on the river. (2001)*

Jep is the baby, and of course they all think he's the spoiled one. It is true that he was born after most of our "bad" years were over. And it is true he went to a private Christian school, which the other boys didn't get to do. And it is true that he's actually the baby. But I don't think he's spoiled! (Well, maybe a little!) As the youngest, he also questioned his spot in the family business. But Jep soon

learned his way around a video camera and now films and edits our Duck Commander hunting videos. Like my other boys, Jep married when he and Jessica were fairly

young. Jessica is always full of energy. She has operated her own "at-home" business for the last several years as well as kept up with their four children. She's learned a little cooking along the way, and like the others, has her recipes we all depend on at family gatherings. She's also our fashionista!

I know most moms would feel blessed with one great daughter-in-law, but I have four! It's so fun to shop and cook and laugh with these amazing women. God knew exactly what my boys needed and He provided!

Green Bean Bundles

Makes 6 servings • 9x13-inch casserole dish (glass, if available) • Small skillet

1 bag (12 ounces) frozen whole green beans

¾ pound thinly sliced bacon, slices cut in half crosswise

1 stick (¼ pound) butter

½ cup packed brown sugar (either light or dark is okay)

Salt and black pepper

Duck Commander Cajun Seasoning (mild or zesty)

Garlic powder

1. Heat the oven to 375°F.

2. Put the green beans in bundles of 4 or 5 each and wrap each bundle with a half-slice of bacon. (You probably won't use all the bacon.) Place the bundles in the casserole dish.

3. In a small skillet, melt the butter over low heat. Stir in the sugar until it melts. *Tip:* This step can also be done in the microwave.

4. Sprinkle salt, pepper, Cajun seasoning, and garlic powder on top of the bundles. Pour the butter-sugar mixture over the bundles. Bake for 45 minutes, or until the bacon is crisp.

A Note from Lisa

This is one of the most delicious ways to cook a vegetable ever! These can be served with the main course or as an appetizer. One of the ladies at our church told me that if she has a really big crowd she's found that cutting the bacon into thirds gives her plenty of bacon to go around. Another friend says she skips the bundles and just puts the beans in a dish, seasons them, pours the butter and sugar on top, and adds some bacon pieces. Sounds good to me!

Chicken & Spaghetti

Makes 8 servings • Large (7- to 8-quart) cooking pot • Medium skillet

1 whole chicken (3½ to 4½ pounds)

1 onion, chopped

2 tablespoons garlic, chopped

1 bell pepper, chopped

1 cup chopped celery

1 stick (¼ pound) butter

1 package (1 pound) spaghetti

1 can (14.75 ounces) cream of
   mushroom soup

1 can (14.75 ounces) cream of chicken
   soup

1 cup shredded cheese (use your
   favorite)

1. In a large pot, cover the chicken with 8 cups of water. Bring to a boil, then turn down the heat and simmer until the chicken is cooked through, about 45 minutes.

2. Lift the chicken out of the pot and set it aside to cool until you can handle it. Save the broth for later use. Remove the skin and bones from the chicken and cut the meat into bite-size pieces.

3. In a large skillet, over medium heat, cook the onion, garlic, bell pepper, and celery in the butter until tender. Add the vegetables to the broth and bring to a boil. Add the spaghetti and cook until tender.

4. Stir in the mushroom soup, cream of chicken soup, and chicken meat. Bring to a boil again.

5. Stir in the cheese for a final touch. *Tip:* If needed, add a can of chicken broth.

A Note from Missy
I love this recipe because it's done almost all in one pot—not much to clean up! Just add a salad and some garlic bread and call everyone to the table.

Fresh Strawberry Pie

Makes 1 (9-inch) pie • Medium saucepan

1 pound fresh strawberries, sliced

¼ cup powdered sugar

1 cup granulated sugar

1 cup water

2½ tablespoons cornstarch

½ teaspoon salt

1 package (6 ounces) strawberry Jell-O

Red food coloring

1 (9-inch) piecrust, homemade (page 182) or store-bought, baked as directed

Whipped topping or fresh whipped cream

1. In a medium bowl, toss the strawberries with the powdered sugar. Let sit for a few minutes, then pour off the juice.

2. While the strawberries are sitting, place the granulated sugar, water, cornstarch, and salt in the saucepan; cook, stirring, until clear and thick, about 3 minutes. Remove from the heat and add ¼ cup of the Jell-O powder and a few drops of red food coloring. Stir well and let cool.

3. Place the strawberries in the piecrust and pour the Jell-O mixture over the strawberries.

4. Top with whipped topping and chill to set before serving.

A Note from Jessica

This is the perfect pie for a hot summer day, and in Louisiana, we have plenty of those! We also have beautiful strawberries grown close to home. We can get them at a farmers' market or the grocery store—either way, they make a great-tasting pie!

Apple Pie

Makes 1 (9-inch) pie • Rolling pin • 9-inch standard pie pan
Pastry blender (Just Google "pastry blender" and see what they look like, then buy one at any store.)

Piecrust

2 cups all-purpose flour, plus more for rolling

1 teaspoon salt

⅔ cup butter-flavored vegetable shortening (I use Crisco)

7 to 10 tablespoons ice water

Pie Filling

6 apples (about 2¼ pounds), peeled, cored, and sliced (I like to use Granny Smith apples)

1 to 1½ cups sugar (depending on how sweet you want it)

¼ teaspoon salt

⅓ cup all-purpose flour

1 teaspoon ground cinnamon

1 tablespoon butter, softened

A Note from Korie

Miss Kay gave me this recipe when I married Willie, and I've used it successfully ever since. And trust me, I'm not the cook in my family, but I can make this!

1. Heat the oven to 350°F.

2. Make the piecrust: In a large bowl, sift the flour and salt together. Add the shortening and mix it in with a pastry blender. Add ice water a tablespoon at a time, stirring with a fork, until the consistency is sticky to the touch but holding together. Divide the dough in half.

3. Place ½ of the dough on floured surface and with a rolling pin, roll it out to a 12-inch round. Put the crust in the pie pan and shape it to the pan. (To make the edge look nice, you can crimp the dough between the thumb and forefinger of one hand and the forefinger of your other hand.)

4. Bake the piecrust at 350°F for 8 minutes, or just until set around the edges. Take it out but leave the oven on.

5. While the crust is baking, in a large bowl, gently mix together the apples, sugar, salt, flour, and cinnamon for the filling.

6. Put the filling into the baked crust. Top the filling with bits of butter.

7. Roll out the second piece of crust to a 12-inch round for the top of the pie. Place it over the filling and turn the edges under the pan. Crimp, if you like. Poke holes in the crust with a fork so it won't bubble up.

8. Bake 45 to 55 minutes, until the top crust is golden brown.

Pecan Chicken

Makes 8 to 12 servings • Cookie sheet • Large skillet • 9 x 13-inch casserole dish

2 cups finely chopped pecans

1 stick of melted butter for pecans

1½ pounds skinless, boneless chicken breast, cut crosswise into ½-inch-wide strips

1½ teaspoons Duck Commander Cajun Seasoning (mild or zesty) or other Cajun seasoning

½ teaspoon salt

½ teaspoon black pepper

½ teaspoon garlic powder

¾ stick (6 tablespoons) butter for chicken

⅓ cup olive oil

⅓ cup packed brown sugar (either light or dark is okay)

⅓ cup maple syrup

1. Heat the oven to 250°F.

2. Arrange the pecans in a single layer on the cookie sheet. Add butter to the top of the pecans. Bake at 250°F for about 15 minutes, until lightly crisped. (Keep a close eye on them; they can burn quickly.) Take the pan out of the oven and turn the oven up to 375°F.

3. Lay the chicken out flat and season with the Cajun seasoning, salt, pepper, and garlic powder.

4. In a large skillet, melt 6 tablespoons butter with the olive oil on medium heat. Add the chicken and cook until lightly browned, about 2 minutes per side. (You may have to cook the chicken in batches.) Transfer the chicken to the casserole dish.

5. Add the sugar and syrup to the skillet and cook for 1 minute, until the sugar melts. Add the pecans and cook for another minute. Pour over the chicken.

6. Cover the casserole with a lid or foil and bake for 12 to 15 minutes, until the chicken is cooked through. Use a fork to test. (The juices should be clear.) *Tip:* The pecans will burn, so watch it carefully.

A Note from Lisa

This is a great recipe for newlyweds. It's a little time-consuming, but not too hard, and it is very impressive! Plus, chicken is one of the cheapest meals to make.

Mexican Cornbread

Makes 16 servings • 2 large cast-iron skillets, or 1 deep skillet for thicker cornbread

10 slices bacon
1½ cups yellow cornmeal
1 can (8.5 ounces) cream-style corn
1 cup buttermilk
½ cup vegetable oil
2 large eggs
1 tablespoon baking powder
1¼ teaspoons salt
2 jalapeño peppers, finely chopped
5 cups shredded cheddar cheese (1¼ pounds)

1. Heat the oven to 350°F.

2. Place 5 slices of bacon in the bottom of each skillet, crisscrossed. (If you're using one deep skillet, use all the bacon.) Put the skillets in the oven so the bacon can start cooking.

3. In a large mixing bowl, put the cornmeal, corn, buttermilk, oil, eggs, baking powder, salt, and jalapeños, in order. Stir well, then add 3 cups of the cheese. Mix together again.

4. Check that you have sufficient bacon grease in the bottom of each skillet. (You need enough grease in the pans to prevent the cornbread from sticking.) If not, add a little extra bacon grease or oil to the bottom and sides of your skillet. Do not remove the bacon from the skillets.

5. Pour equal amounts of batter into the skillets, over the bacon. Bake for 45 minutes.

6. Sprinkle 1 cup of cheese on top of the cornbread in each skillet. If you chose to use one skillet, top with cheese as desired.

7. Bake for 15 minutes more, until the cheese is melted and lightly browned.

8. Run a spatula under the edges and around the sides of the skillets to loosen the bread. Flip the bread onto a plate so that the bacon is on top.

A Note from Lisa

I love to cook and have gathered recipes from Miss Kay and many other mentor moms over my life. This recipe originally came to Miss Kay through Shirley Riley, a friend and neighbor down on the river. I added the bacon for a richer, more fattening effect! Enjoy!

Mozzarella Chicken

Makes 2 to 4 servings • Medium nonstick skillet • 9 x 13-inch casserole dish • Blender

2 tablespoons butter
½ teaspoon garlic powder
4 small skinless, boneless chicken
    breast halves (5 to 6 ounces each)
2 cups finely chopped fresh tomatoes
½ teaspoon Italian seasoning
1 cup shredded mozzarella cheese
4 teaspoons grated Parmesan cheese

1. Heat the oven to 350°F.

2. In the skillet, melt the butter over medium heat. Stir in the garlic powder (adjust according to your taste).

3. Add the chicken and cook until lightly browned, about 2 minutes per side. Transfer the chicken to the casserole dish.

4. In a blender, puree the tomatoes and Italian seasoning. Pour over the chicken. Top the chicken with the mozzarella and Parmesan. Bake until the chicken is cooked through and the cheese has melted, about 25 minutes. Use a fork to test. (The juices should be clear.)

A Note from Korie
Of course, as your family grows, this recipe can grow, too. Just add more chicken and more of everything else! This is another great newlywed recipe.

Fried Pies

Makes 12 pies • Rolling pin • Deep heavy pot
Pastry blender (Just Google "pastry blender" and see what they look like, then buy one at any store.)

5 cups all-purpose flour, plus more for rolling and pressing

2 teaspoons sugar

1 teaspoon baking powder

1 teaspoon salt

1¾ cups butter-flavored vegetable shortening (I use Crisco)

1 can (12 ounces) evaporated milk (I use Pet)

1 large egg

One 14-ounce can pie filling your choice (apple is our favorite)

Vegetable or canola oil, for deep-frying

Powdered sugar, for sprinkling

1. In a large mixing bowl, sift together the flour, sugar, baking powder, and salt. With the pastry blender, cut in the shortening. Add the milk and mix well. Add the egg and gently mix. Cover the bowl and put in the refrigerator to chill for 1 hour.

2. Working with half of the dough (keep the rest in the fridge), place it on a floured surface and roll it out to about ⅛ inch thick. Cut into saucer-size circles (about 6 inches in diameter). Put a small amount of pie filling (about 1½ tablespoons) in the center of the dough. Fold the sides together to make a half-moon and crimp the edges together with a fork dipped in flour. Repeat with the rest of the dough and filling.

3. Fill the pot halfway with oil and turn the heat on medium. Heat the oil to 350°F. (Drop a pinch of flour in the oil to check the temperature. The flour will sizzle when it's ready.)

4. Carefully place a few pies at a time in the hot oil and deep-fry until brown, turning once during cooking. The pies will float to the top when done. Place on paper towels to drain. Sprinkle with powdered sugar to serve.

A Note from Jessica

This is one of the dishes I love for Miss Kay to cook. Kay uses apples and peaches the most, but apples are my favorite.

Hot Spinach Dip

Makes 6 to 8 servings • Microwave • Microwave-safe bowl
9-inch square baking pan (glass is prettier, but any will do)

2 packages (9 or 10 ounces) frozen chopped spinach, thawed and drained

1 stick (¼ pound) butter, softened

1 package (8 ounces) cream cheese, softened

1 container (8 ounces) sour cream

1 package (1.4 ounces) Knorr Vegetable Recipe Mix

2 cups freshly shredded Parmesan cheese

Duck Commander Cajun Seasoning (mild or zesty)

Wheat Thins crackers or tortilla chips, for serving

1. Heat the oven to 350°F.

2. Combine the spinach and butter and cook in the microwave until warmed all the way through.

3. In a separate bowl, whisk the cream cheese and sour cream until well blended. Add the vegetable mix and 1 cup of the Parmesan cheese. Fold in the spinach and mix all together. Add Cajun seasoning to taste. Pour into the baking dish. Top with the rest of the cheese and more Cajun seasoning, as desired.

4. Bake for 20 minutes, or until the cheese begins to brown.

5. Serve hot with crackers or tortilla chips.

A Note from Missy

We have lots of showers, both bridal and baby, at our large church, and I love to host them in my home. This is a great recipe for a shower or as an appetizer for any dinner party.

4.

When the Grandkids Come Over

~~~~~~~~~~~~~~~~~~~~~~~~~~~~

Grandmas never run out

of hugs or cookies.

—Author Unknown

One day children were brought to Jesus in the hope that he would lay hands on them and pray over them. The disciples shooed them off. But Jesus intervened: "Let the children alone, don't prevent them from coming to me. God's kingdom is made up of people like these."

—Matthew 19:13–15, *The Message*

Recipes for the Grandkids

〰〰〰〰〰〰〰〰〰〰〰〰〰〰〰〰〰〰〰〰

Biscuits & Cupcakes

As you know by now, I have four boys and, oh, they were rough. Our small house was a maze of baseball gloves, basketballs, footballs, and comic books. As much as I loved raising those boys, I was ready for a little girl when my first granddaughter came along. She was premature and the tiniest thing I had ever seen. She weighed just under two pounds—not much bigger than a little squirrel! I had so much fun buying pink frilly dresses and books with ballerinas on the front.

Alan and Lisa gave me my first two granddaughters, but God must have heard my request for more, as six more granddaughters were added to our family. Plus, now I have two great-granddaughters! That's ten girls! My two oldest granddaughters are married now, but my house is still filled with feather boas, tiny tea sets, and princess costumes—it's so much fun!

Now, I love my grandsons, too! It's great to see them growing up—some of them are already young men—and they make me so proud. Cole, Reed, John Luke, Will, and River love coming over, too; but they're not as interested in cooking as the little girls are. And cooking with my granddaughters is one of the things I love the most.

Above: *Our family goes to the beach every summer. We rent a large house so we can all be together. It's so much fun. These are all my grandchildren and great-grandchildren. I think they're pretty cute! (2012)*

I want to pass on my love for cooking, so every time they visit we make something. Biscuits are a grandkid favorite and our tiniest, but not the youngest, one, Mia, can eat five at a time! Bella loves biscuits, too, but I tell her she has more butter than biscuit when she finishes stuffing it with a huge pat of butter. Lily asks for hers to be "just like Bella's," so the more butter, the better for those two girls. I think they're onto something.

Biscuits are great, but Merritt loves cupcakes. One day we made a batch of cupcakes and iced them with chocolate frosting. The plan was to wait until after lunch to eat them. But somebody got hungry! I looked at all of the girls and noticed the telltale sign of sneaking a bite on Merritt's face. I said, "Merritt, did you get hungry and take a bite of a cupcake?" She was only two years old at the time, but she realized she had been caught. All I could do was laugh at her cute face covered in chocolate icing.

Gather up your girls and teach them how to cook, but more important, show them your unconditional love. I know my own kids made mistakes and my grandkids will, too, but I will always love them. When children grow up in an environment where their parents and grandparents love them and lead them, they have a better chance of battling the pressures of the world. Love them and lead them with your example in and out of the kitchen! 🦆

Above: Korie's mom hosts our big Easter celebration each year. After raising those boys, I sure love being surrounded by pretty little girls in their Easter dresses. (2012)

Homemade Pancakes

Makes 4 servings • Electric griddle or large cast-iron griddle or skillet

1¼ cups all-purpose flour, sifted

2½ teaspoons baking powder

2 tablespoons sugar

¾ teaspoon salt

1 large egg

1¼ cups milk

3 tablespoon butter or other fat, melted, or vegetable oil, plus more for the griddle (optional)

Oil or nonstick cooking spray, for the griddle (optional)

Softened butter, for serving

1. In a large bowl, sift together the flour, baking powder, sugar, and salt. In a separate bowl, stir together the egg, milk, and melted butter. Combine the wet and dry ingredients (batter will be lumpy).

2. Set an electric griddle to 350°F or heat a cast-iron griddle or skillet on medium heat. Lightly grease the griddle with your choice of fat. The griddle will be hot enough for cooking when water drops dance on it.

3. With a large spoon, measuring cup, or ladle, pour batter on the griddle. (The size you make the pancakes can vary from silver-dollar-size to saucer-size. You decide.) Cook one side until the batter bubbles up, then flip or turn with a spatula. Cook 2 minutes more, until the bottom is golden.

4. Stack on a plate with butter between the pancakes.

A Note from Miss Kay

Pancakes are such a family favorite that our griddle goes with us on vacation. Korie's son, Will, loves to "flip" our pancakes. I think we have another cook in the family! One of the cooks at church used my recipe and added mini chocolate chips. She said her family loved it! Great idea!

Hot Waffles

Makes 8 waffles • Electric waffle iron • Electric mixer

1½ cups all-purpose flour

1 tablespoon baking powder

½ teaspoon salt

2 large eggs, separated

2 teaspoons sugar

1½ cups milk

½ stick (4 tablespoons) butter, melted (margarine or ¼ cup vegetable oil can be substituted)

1. Plug in the waffle iron and let it heat up.

2. In a large bowl, sift the flour, baking powder, and salt together. (If you don't have a sifter, just mix them well.)

3. Beat the egg yolks and sugar in a separate bowl.

4. Add the milk and melted butter to the flour. Add the egg yolks and sugar and stir slowly.

5. Beat the egg whites with the mixer until stiff peaks form. (The peaks will stay standing when you remove the beaters.) Fold into the batter.

6. Pour batter into the center lower half of the waffle iron, until it spreads about 1 inch from the edges. Bring the cover down gently. Cook as your waffle iron directs. Serve hot from the waffle iron.

A Note from Miss Kay

Waffles are another family favorite and the waffle iron goes on vacation with us just like the griddle does. That's right—no rest for this cook! But I love it when all my sleepy family appears for breakfast.

Grandma's Chocolate Chip Cookies

Makes about 48 cookies • Electric mixer • Cookie sheets • Wire cooling racks

2 sticks (½ pound) butter or
  margarine, softened
¾ cup granulated sugar
¾ cup packed brown sugar (either
  light or dark is okay)
1 large egg
2¼ cups all-purpose flour
1 teaspoon baking soda
½ teaspoon salt
1 cup coarsely chopped pecans
2 cups semisweet chocolate chips
  (12-ounce package)

1. Heat the oven to 375°F.

2. With the electric mixer, beat the butter, sugars, and egg until creamy.

3. Sift together the flour, baking soda, and salt. Add to the butter mixture and stir in (the dough will be stiff). By hand, stir in the nuts and chocolate chips. Drop the dough by rounded tablespoonfuls onto ungreased cookie sheets, about 2 inches apart.

4. Bake 8 to 10 minutes, until light brown (the centers will be soft).

5. Cool slightly on the cookie sheets. Remove from the cookie sheets to cooling racks or a platter for serving.

A Note from Miss Kay

A grandma's cookie jar can never be too full. This recipe makes about four dozen, so doubling it might be a good idea. That way you always have enough. It is pretty much the Ultimate Chocolate Chip Cookie recipe found in the Betty Crocker cookbook and on their website. I have been using it for years and don't think anyone can improve on it. It's great with or without nuts, depending on the folks eating them.

Homemade Mac & Cheese

Makes 8 servings • Medium saucepan • 9x13-inch casserole dish

1 package (1 pound) large elbow
  macaroni
1 stick plus 1 tablespoon (9
  tablespoons) butter
Salt and black pepper
9 tablespoons all-purpose flour
3 cups milk
2 cups shredded cheddar cheese

1. Heat the oven to 350°F. Cook the macaroni according to package directions.

2. While the macaroni is boiling, melt the butter in the saucepan on medium heat. Add salt and pepper and the flour, stirring continuously. When thoroughly combined, slowly stir in the milk. Stir until it thickens, then turn off the heat.

3. Drain the macaroni and pour into the casserole dish. Cover with sauce. Add 1½ cups of the cheese and mix all together. Sprinkle the remaining cheese on top.

4. Bake until the cheese has melted and the macaroni is hot.

A Note from Miss Kay

Most kids love a good mac and cheese, but it's likely they're used to the packaged kind. This is really an easy recipe, so give it a try. Even my self-proclaimed noncook, Korie, can make this mac and cheese!

Willie's Famous Chicken Strips

Makes 2 to 3 servings • Large cast-iron skillet • Deep-fry thermometer

1 large egg

½ cup buttermilk

1 cup all-purpose flour

1 tablespoon Duck Commander Cajun Seasoning (mild or zesty) or other Cajun seasoning

1½ teaspoons garlic powder

1 teaspoon salt

1 teaspoon black pepper

½ teaspoon paprika

1 cup vegetable oil

1 pound chicken tenderloins or skinless, boneless chicken breasts, cut crosswise into ½-inch-wide strips

1. In a small bowl, whisk together the egg and buttermilk. In another bowl, combine the flour, Cajun seasoning, garlic powder, salt, pepper, and paprika.

2. Heat the oil in the skillet to 375°F on medium-high heat.

3. A few at a time, dip the chicken pieces in the egg mixture and then in the flour mixture. Cook for 2 minutes on each side, or until no longer pink inside. Drain on paper towels.

A Note from Miss Kay
If you can't beat 'em, join 'em! The kids love chicken strips from any fast-food place, but they can't be better than these homemade ones. The grandkids love these, but so do my big kids. This is one of Willie's favorite dishes.

Above: *The school my grandkids go to puts on a production for the grandparents every year. Little Will got to play big Willie in the 2012 production. He nailed it!*

Hamburger Steak

Makes 4 to 6 servings • Large skillet

1½ pounds hamburger meat

1 large egg

⅓ cup evaporated milk (I use Pet)

1 tablespoon Worcestershire sauce

1 onion, chopped

Salt and black pepper

Duck Commander Cajun Seasoning
  (mild or zesty) or other Cajun
  seasoning

All-purpose flour, to coat

1 to 1½ cups peanut oil, for frying

1. In a large bowl, combine the meat, egg, milk, Worcestershire, onion, salt and pepper (we like it heavy on the pepper side), and Cajun seasoning. Mix with your hands to combine. Pat into thick patties (you decide how many). Coat the patties with flour.

2. Pour enough oil into the skillet to come up 2 inches, and heat on medium-high.

3. Fry the patties quickly in the hot oil, turning them halfway through. Turn the heat down if the patties are browning too quickly.

4. Mash lightly with a fork to test if the patties are done. (The juices should be clear.)

A Note from Miss Kay

If you have some young cooks, this is a great one to let them help. They love mixing up the ground meat and making it into patties. You can use a small saucer to smash your hamburger steak into a perfect round shape or just smash with your hands. I call that freestyle!

Melt-in-Your-Mouth Biscuits

Makes about 20 (3-inch) biscuits • Rolling pin
Pastry blender (You can just Google "pastry blender" and see what they look like, then buy one at any store.)
2 cast-iron skillets, baking sheet with ½-inch sides, or 9x13-inch casserole dish

4 cups biscuit mix (I use Pioneer), plus more for rolling
2 cups sour cream
1 partial can 7Up or Sprite (about ¼ cup)
½ stick (4 tablespoons) butter

1. Heat the oven to 375°F.

2. In a large bowl, mix together the biscuit mix and the sour cream with a pastry blender. Add 7Up a little at a time and mix with a fork until the dough forms a ball. (You will not need the whole can. Don't overdo the liquid.)

3. Sprinkle about ½ cup of biscuit mix on the counter to roll the dough in. Turn the dough out onto the biscuit mix on the counter. The dough will be wet, so pat on a little more biscuit mix as needed. With a rolling pin, roll the dough to ½ inch thick.

4. Melt the butter in the skillets or baking pan.

5. Using a round biscuit cutter, cut out the biscuits. (A small drinking glass will also do.) Dip the cutter in biscuit mix first for easier cutting.

6. Dip both sides of each biscuit in the melted butter and place the biscuits close together in the pan.

7. Bake for 20 minutes, or until golden brown.

A Note from Miss Kay
This recipe will make two pans of biscuits, which we always need. Phil makes jelly for our family, which is perfect with biscuits. Yes, ladies, he definitely does more than hunt!

Missy's Twice-Baked Potatoes

Makes 6 to 8 servings • Microwave • Gallon-size resealable plastic bag • Large microwave-safe bowl

8 or 9 medium russet (baking) potatoes (about 2½ pounds)

1 stick (¼ pound) butter

1 package (1 ounce) ranch dressing mix (I use Hidden Valley)

1⅓ to 1½ cups milk

2 cups shredded Colby-Jack cheese

½ cup chopped green onions or scallions (leave out if your family doesn't like onions)

1 package (4.3 ounces) real bacon pieces (not imitation bacon bits!)

Duck Commander Cajun Seasoning (mild or zesty)

1. Scrub the potatoes. Use a sharp knife to poke two holes through each potato. Place all potatoes in the plastic bag, close it, and cook in the microwave on high for 20 minutes, or until done (poke the potatoes with a fork to check).

2. Place the butter in the bowl and set aside.

3. While the potatoes are still hot (hold them with a pot holder), cut them in half. Scoop the potato out of the skin and into the bowl with the butter. Discard the skins.

4. Pour the ranch mix onto the potatoes, then add milk. With a potato masher or fork, mash the potatoes until they are creamy and have absorbed all the milk. Stir, making sure the ranch mix is all blended through. Stir in 1 cup of the cheese, ¼ cup of the green onions, ½ the package of bacon, and Cajun seasoning to taste until all is mixed together. Top with the rest of the cheese, onions, and bacon pieces. Shake on more Cajun seasoning to taste.

5. Cook in the microwave on high for 4 to 5 minutes, until the cheese is completely melted.

A Note from Missy

This is a great recipe for a crowd; and any time our family gets together, it's a crowd. The kids love it!

Papaw Phil's Homemade Ice Cream

Makes about 3 quarts • Electric mixer • 4-quart ice cream maker • Crushed ice and rock salt (optional)

2 cups heavy whipping cream

1½ cups granulated sugar

7 large eggs

1 can (14 ounces) sweetened condensed milk (I use Eagle Brand)

1 can (12 ounces) evaporated milk (I use Pet)

Pinch of salt

1½ tablespoons vanilla extract

1⅓ cups powdered sugar

2 cups half-and-half

About 1 cup whole milk (enough to bring mixture to the top of the freezer)

1. With the electric mixer, beat the whipping cream with half the granulated sugar until soft peaks form. (The peaks should be able to stand and bend over as you remove the beaters.)

2. In another large bowl, beat the eggs with the rest of the granulated sugar until fluffy. Adding each ingredient one at a time, beat in the condensed milk, evaporated milk, salt, vanilla, and powdered sugar.

3. Put into the ice cream maker canister. Add the whipped cream mixture, then the half-and-half. Add the whole milk until the mixture is only 4 or 5 inches from the top of the canister.

4. Freeze as directed using ice and rock salt, or if your freezer doesn't require ice and rock salt, just follow the manufacturer's directions.

A Note from Phil

I learned how to cook at an early age and I enjoy cooking with Miss Kay. This is a recipe the whole family loves. It's perfect for a hot summer day.

Nutty Good Oatmeal Cookies

Makes about 48 cookies • Electric mixer • Cookie sheets • Wire cooling racks

2 sticks (½ pound) butter, softened

1 cup packed brown sugar (either light or dark is okay)

1 cup granulated sugar

2 large eggs

1 teaspoon vanilla extract

2 cups all-purpose flour

1 teaspoon baking soda

1 teaspoon salt

½ teaspoon baking powder

2 cups rolled oats

1 cup chocolate chips (6-ounce package)

½ cup chopped pecans

1. Heat the oven to 350°F.

2. With the electric mixer, beat the butter, sugars, eggs, and vanilla until creamy. In a large bowl, sift together the flour, baking soda, salt, and baking powder. Beat the flour into the butter mixture until well combined.

3. By hand, stir in the oats, chocolate chips, and pecans. (The dough will be very thick. Use your muscles!)

4. Drop by large spoonfuls onto ungreased cookie sheets.

5. Bake for 12 to 14 minutes, until set. Cool for 5 minutes on the cookie sheets, then transfer to wire racks to cool completely.

A Note from Miss Kay

I keep a cookie jar on my counter at all times! I notice as many adults reaching in as I do children. There's just something about a full cookie jar that says, "I love you."

5.

Company's Coming

〜〜〜〜〜〜〜〜〜〜〜〜〜〜〜

When company leaves, never say anything negative about how much they ate. They loved your cooking!

—Phil Robertson

Most of all, love each other as if your life depended on it. Love makes up for practically anything. Be quick to give a meal to the hungry, a bed to the homeless—cheerfully. Be generous with the different things God gave you, passing them around so all get in on it: if words, let it be God's words; if help, let it be God's hearty help.

—1 Peter 4:8–10, *The Message*

Recipes for When Company Comes

〜〜〜〜〜〜〜〜〜〜〜〜〜〜〜〜〜〜〜〜〜〜〜〜〜〜〜

Frying Fish

Phil and his brothers grew up challenging each other in everything, and one of those things was football. But it paid off, as Phil went to Louisiana Tech on a full football scholarship. His older brother, Tommy, and Tommy's wife, Nancy, were already at Tech. Tommy had received a football scholarship the year before Phil got his.

I still don't know how I did it, but I finished my senior year at Ruston High School while married to my football hero and pregnant. We lived on the university campus in the same housing complex as Tommy and Nancy. I loved having some family close by. They were both a big help to me that year—especially after I had Alan. Plus, it made newly married life more fun.

We all loved to eat fish, and it was a cheap meal. Tommy and Phil loved to fish along the Ouachita River and Lake D'Arbonne and usually caught the limit, which was fifteen at the time. But to fry fish, you have to have oil, and oil was way too expensive for us college students on limited

Above: In the early years, I cooked every day for our whole Duck Commander crew—who worked at our house. Now I take meals to the warehouse from time to time. Everyone loves a home-cooked meal!

budgets. So Tommy, Phil, Nancy, and I would pool our money and buy oil to share. We kept it in the big cast-iron pan that we fried the fish in, and every week you would see us hauling that iron pot from our house to their house and vice versa. We would do this until the oil went bad, then we would buy some new oil and start over. I know the other students thought we were crazy carrying that heavy pot from house to house.

Family is where we first learn about sharing, getting along in a community of people, and being hospitable. That oil stands as a symbol for working together for the good of everyone. I'm so thankful that we had Tommy and Nancy in our early years. I cherish the time we spent together as young couples. No matter what stage of life you're in, learn something from everyone you meet. You can't do that if you keep your doors shut. Open your door to visitors. Most people don't even care what you cook or if you have enough; mostly they just need a listening ear. You'll be surprised what you can teach others, and you'll be surprised what they can teach you.

Opposite: No matter who comes to dinner, Phil is sure to preach a little. Over the years, Phil has given countless people, young and old, sound advice for living right.

Smoked Ham with Sweet & Sassy Glaze

A 7-pound half-ham serves around 12 • Roasting pan

2 jalapeño peppers

1½ cups packed brown sugar (either light or dark is okay)

½ teaspoon ground ginger

1 can (15.5 ounces) crushed pineapple in juice, drained, reserving the juice

Smoked ham of your choice

1. Heat the oven to 350°F.

2. Remove the stems from the jalapeños and finely chop them along with their seeds.

3. In a medium saucepan, combine the brown sugar, ginger, jalapeños and seeds, and crushed pineapple. Cook on medium heat, stirring until sugar begins to melt. If necessary, add some of the reserved pineapple juice to thin the glaze just a bit. The consistency should be slightly thicker than syrup.

4. Put the ham in the roasting pan. Pour the glaze over it and bake for 1 hour.

> *Tip* Make double the amount of glaze and reserve half to use as a table sauce for the ham.

A Note from Miss Kay

Phil thinks the photo on the opposite page makes me look "sweet and sassy" like this ham. That's the way I like it.

Alan's Corn Chowder

Makes about 4 quarts • Small casserole dish • Large skillet • Large saucepan • Large (7- to 8-quart) cooking pot

2 pounds russet (baking) potatoes, peeled and cut into chunks

¾ pound smoked sausage (we prefer Savoie's andouille)

1 bell pepper, finely chopped

1 white onion, finely chopped

1 celery stalk, finely chopped

1 garlic clove, finely chopped

1 stick (¼ pound) butter

1 package (1 pound) frozen hash brown potatoes

1 pound frozen whole kernel corn

Salt and black pepper

1–2 cans (12 ounces) evaporated milk

2 cups whole milk

Grated cheese, for serving

Crackers of your choice, for serving

1. In a large pot, bring 6 cups of water to a boil. Cook the russet potatoes until just soft but not mushy; drain. Heat the oven to 250°F. Cut the sausage into small pieces and brown on a cookie sheet in the oven for 20 minutes. Drain the grease off on paper towels.

2. While the sausage is browning, in a large skillet, cook bell pepper, onion, celery, and garlic in the butter until they become very soft.

3. Bring 6 cups of water to a boil in the large pot. Add the hash brown and russet potatoes, corn, softened vegetables, sausage, and salt and black pepper to taste. Bring the soup back to a boil, lower to a simmer, and cook for 1 hour, until thickened.

4. Stir in the evaporated and whole milk and simmer until the soup is piping hot.

5. Serve topped with grated or small chunks of cheese, and crackers.

A Note from Alan

This recipe seems like a lot of ingredients and a lot of chopping, but it's really pretty easy to make and is great for company. Lisa and I love to cook together, so she can be working on another part of the meal while I work on all the chopping.

Corn Shrimp Soup

Makes about 5 quarts • Large (7- to 8-quart) cooking pot with a lid

⅓ cup olive oil

2 onions, chopped

1 bell pepper, chopped

2 celery stalks, chopped

6 green onions or scallions, chopped, white and green parts separated

½ to 1 teaspoon Duck Commander Cajun Seasoning (mild or zesty)

1 can (64 ounces) V8 juice (regular or spicy)

1 bottle (32 ounces) bloody Mary mix

2 pounds fresh medium shrimp

1 can (15.25 ounces) whole kernel corn

1 tube (20 ounces) frozen creamed corn (Melissa uses McKenzie's), or 2 cans (one 14.75 ounces and one 8.5 ounces) cream-style corn

Salt and black pepper

Just Right White Rice (page 110), for serving

1. In the pot, heat the oil on medium heat. Add the onion, bell pepper, celery, and white part of the green onions. Cook, stirring occasionally, until the onions are translucent, about 8 minutes.

2. Add Cajun seasoning to taste and stir to coat. Pour in the juice and bloody Mary mix. Bring to a boil, lower to a simmer, cover with the lid, and cook on medium-low heat for 1 hour.

3. While the soup is simmering, peel and devein the shrimp. Put them on ice in a bowl in the refrigerator to keep cool. (Five or six pieces of ice will do it.)

4. Add the corn kernels and creamed corn to the soup. Simmer for 30 minutes, stirring frequently. If you're using canned creamed corn, just simmer until the soup is nice and hot again.

5. Add the shrimp with melted ice and green part of the green onions and bring back to a simmer. Cook just until the shrimp turn pink. Stir in salt and black pepper to taste.

6. Serve hot, over rice.

A Note from Miss Kay

I love this recipe from my niece Melissa Atkins. She is the daughter of Phil's younger sister, Jan. It's perfect for a house full of company. Thanks for sharing, Melissa.

Broiled Asparagus

Makes 4 servings • Cookie sheet

1 large bunch asparagus (about
   1 pound)
Pinch of garlic powder or garlic salt
Pinch of Duck Commander Cajun
   Seasoning (mild or zesty) or other
   Cajun seasoning
Salt and black pepper
¼ cup olive oil

1. Wash the asparagus to remove any dirt that may be lodged in the tips or stuck to the stalks. (Remember, this is a "straight out of the ground" vegetable.) Snap off the bottoms of the asparagus stalks; that part of the stalk is not very good to eat. Just grab the bottom and bend it. It should snap at a natural breaking point. This will be the tender spot close to the end.

2. Set the oven to broil.

3. Spread the asparagus on the cookie sheet in a single layer. Sprinkle with the garlic powder, Cajun seasoning, and salt and pepper to taste. Drizzle a small amount of olive oil on each spear.

4. Broil 8 to 10 minutes, turning once, until the asparagus is lightly browned and tender. Use a sharp knife to test for tenderness. Broil a few more minutes if necessary. The timing will vary depending on the thickness of the asparagus.

A Note from Miss Kay

Asparagus is one of the easiest vegetables to make, but it looks fancy. It can be prepared several different ways, and all are good. You don't read about broiling asparagus often, but I tried it one day and loved it. So did everyone else!

Classic Banana Cream Pie

Makes 1 (9-inch) pie

3 tablespoons cornstarch

1⅔ cups water

1 can (14 ounces) sweetened condensed milk (I use Eagle Brand)

3 large egg yolks, lightly beaten

2 tablespoons butter

1 teaspoon vanilla extract

3 medium bananas

Lemon juice

1 (9-inch) piecrust, homemade (page 182) or store-bought, baked as directed

Whipped cream or whipped topping

1. In a saucepan, dissolve the cornstarch in the water. Stir in the condensed milk and egg yolks. Cook on medium heat, stirring continuously, until thickened and bubbly. Be careful not to burn it. Remove from heat; stir in the butter and vanilla. Cool slightly.

2. Slice two of the bananas into coins; lightly dip in lemon juice to prevent rounds from discoloring. Arrange the banana slices on the bottom of the piecrust. Pour the filling over the bananas. Cover and chill for 4 hours or until set.

3. Top the pie with whipped cream. Slice the remaining banana, dip in lemon juice, drain, and garnish the top of the pie.

A Note from Miss Kay

In case you don't know this, dipping fruit (bananas or apples) in lemon juice will keep them looking fresh. But dip quickly and lightly so the lemon taste doesn't take over your pie or salad. Enjoy!

Jay's Duck Commander Ribs

Makes 2 to 3 servings • Baking sheet with ½-inch sides • Outdoor grill

1 squeeze bottle (12 ounces) butter spread

1 bottle (5 ounces) Try Me Tiger Sauce (found online or in grocery stores)

1 full rack ribs (about 3 pounds)

1 packet (5 ounces) Duck Commander Seasoning Rub, or any rub you like

Onion powder

1 bottle (about 20 ounces) BBQ sauce of your choice

1. Heat the oven to 200°F. Tear off two pieces of foil, each large enough to wrap the rack of ribs. Then place one on top of the other on the counter to make a double layer. Turn up the edges a little to make a rim.

2. Put a generous portion of the butter spread and Tiger sauce on the foil. Season the ribs with the rub and place them on the foil, meaty side down. Close the packet and crimp the foil to seal. Place on the baking sheet. Bake 3 hours to 3 hours and 30 minutes, until the ribs are tender enough to be pierced with a knife when you open the foil package.

3. When the ribs are almost done, heat an outdoor grill set up for indirect heat.

4. Dust the ribs lightly with onion powder. Place the ribs, bone side down, on the grill. Glaze with BBQ sauce and cook for approximately 30 minutes. The ribs are cooked already—this is just to give them a smoky taste.

5. Glaze with more Tiger Sauce and butter spread right before serving.

A Note from Jay

Grilling out is an easy and delicious way to cook almost anything. It's often hot in Louisiana, but that doesn't stop us guys from hanging out around the grill. I like hickory chips to get that perfect "cooked out" taste. An added bonus is not having many dishes to do when supper is done. Anna likes that part. (Anna is Alan's daughter, and Jay is her husband.)

Baked Mushroom-Soup Chicken

Makes 4 to 6 servings • Large skillet • Dutch oven or 9x13-inch casserole dish

1 chicken (3½ to 4½ pounds), cut up, or purchase just the parts your family eats

1½ teaspoons Duck Commander Cajun Seasoning (mild or zesty)

1 teaspoon salt

½ teaspoon black pepper

3 tablespoons vegetable oil

2 cans (4½ ounces each) sliced mushrooms

2 cans (10.75 ounces each) cream of mushroom soup

1 onion, peeled and quartered

1. Heat the oven to 350°F.

2. Rub the chicken pieces with the Cajun seasoning, salt, and pepper. In a large skillet, heat the oil over medium heat. When hot, cook the chicken until browned, about 3 minutes per side. Work in batches, if necessary. Transfer the browned chicken to the Dutch oven or casserole dish.

3. Add the mushrooms, mushroom soup, and onion. Cover with the Dutch oven lid or foil. Bake for 1 hour and 15 minutes or until the chicken is cooked through. Use a fork to test. (The juices should be clear.)

A Note from Miss Kay

This is a simple recipe, but in today's busy world, simple is good. Right? Our family is so big that each chicken part is somebody's favorite, but if your family just likes dark meat, just use dark meat. This is great served with rice, boiled red potatoes, or mashed potatoes. The soup acts as a gravy.

Hummingbird Cake with Cream Cheese Frosting

Makes 1 (9-inch) cake • 3 (9-inch) round cake pans • Wire cooling racks
Nonstick cooking spray and flour, for the pans

Cake Layers

1½ cups canola or vegetable oil
2 cups granulated sugar
3 large eggs, lightly beaten
1½ teaspoons vanilla extract
1 teaspoon baking soda
1 teaspoon ground cinnamon
½ teaspoon salt
3 cups all-purpose flour
2 cups diced bananas
1 can (8 ounces) crushed pineapple
   with juice
1 cup chopped pecans

Cream Cheese Frosting

1 stick (¼ pound) butter, softened
1 package (8 ounces) cream cheese,
   softened
1 teaspoon vanilla extract
1 package (1 pound) powdered sugar
1 cup chopped pecans

1. Heat the oven to 350°F. Grease and flour the cake pans.

2. Make the cake layers: In a large bowl, stir together the oil, sugar, eggs, and vanilla by hand. Add the baking soda, cinnamon, salt, and flour. Mix well by hand. Stir in the bananas, pineapple with juice, and pecans.

3. Pour the batter into the pans. Bake until the layers start to pull away at the sides and a toothpick inserted in the center of a layer comes out clean, 25 to 30 minutes.

4. Let the layers cool in the pans for a few minutes, then run a spatula around the sides and invert the layers onto a wire rack to cool completely.

5. While the layers are cooling, make the frosting: Beat together the butter, cream cheese, vanilla, and sugar until fluffy. (The frosting will appear stiff at first, but will soften as you mix.)

6. When the cake layers are cool, frost the top of one layer. Put another layer on top and frost that layer. Put the last layer on top and frost the top and sides. Sprinkle with the pecans.

A Note from Miss Kay

To make this cake more delicious, I double the frosting recipe and put more pecans and frosting between each layer and on top. Hummingbird cake is very popular in the South because southern folks love their pecans. If you need to keep this cake fresh, store it in the refrigerator. At the Robertson house there's no need to do this, because it's all eaten the first time it's put out.

Banana Nut Cake with Caramel Icing

Makes 1 (9-inch) cake • 2 (9-inch) round cake pans • Electric mixer • Butter and flour, for the cake pans

Cake Layers

2½ cups sifted cake flour (I use Soft as Silk), or 2 cups all-purpose flour

1⅔ cups sugar

1¼ teaspoons baking powder

1¼ teaspoons baking soda

1 teaspoon salt

⅔ cup vegetable shortening (I use Crisco)

⅓ cup buttermilk

1 cup mashed bananas (about 2 medium bananas)

2 large eggs

⅔ cup chopped pecans or walnuts

Caramel Icing

1 stick (¼ pound) butter

1 cup packed brown sugar (either light or dark is okay)

⅓ cup milk

3½ cups sifted powdered sugar

1. Heat the oven to 350°F. Butter and flour the cake pans.

2. Make the cake layers: In a large mixing bowl, sift together the flour, sugar, baking powder, baking soda, and salt. Add the shortening, buttermilk, and bananas. Mix with the electric mixer on medium speed for 2 minutes. Add the eggs and beat 2 minutes more. Fold in the nuts.

3. Pour the batter into the pans. Bake until the layers start to pull away at the sides and a toothpick inserted in the center of a layer comes out clean, 35 to 40 minutes.

4. Let the layers cool in the pans for a few minutes, then run a spatula around the sides and invert the layers onto a wire rack to cool completely.

5. While the layers are cooling, make the frosting: In a medium saucepan on medium heat, bring the butter and brown sugar to a boil and boil for 2 minutes. Add the milk and bring back to a boil. Remove from the heat and let cool slightly. Stir in the powdered sugar.

6. When the cake layers are cool, frost the top of one layer. Put the other layer on top and frost the top and sides.

A Note from Miss Kay

This is about the "moistest" cake I make. It takes a little effort, but it's definitely worth it. Try it, you'll like it!

Guacamole

Makes 6 servings

3 or 4 Hass avocados
3 tomatoes, chopped
1 small onion, finely chopped
3 tablespoons chopped cilantro
Chopped jalapeño pepper (1 is
  probably plenty)
Juice from 1 lime
Salt and black pepper

Cut avocados in half lengthwise and remove the pits. Use a spoon to scoop out the meat of the avocados and place in a medium bowl. Mash up the avocados with a fork. Add the tomatoes, onion, cilantro, jalapeño, lime juice, and salt and pepper to taste. Stir to combine.

Tip Picking avocados for guacamole can be tricky. Just look for the ones with a darker shell that are soft to the touch. If the avocados are hard, place them in a brown paper bag and keep them on the kitchen counter for a day or two and they'll soften.

A Note from Miss Kay
We love to try other recipes and this is from Karyna, one of the young ladies on the film crew. Phil loved teasing her about coming from Mexico, but she was actually born in the United States. However, her family is from Mexico so you know this has to be a good guacamole recipe. We certainly like it.

6.

Louisiana at Its Best!

〜〜〜〜〜〜〜〜〜〜〜〜〜〜〜〜〜〜〜〜〜〜

Part of the secret of success in life is to eat what you like and let the food fight it out inside.

—Mark Twain

When you enter a town and are welcomed, eat what is offered to you.

—Luke 10:8, NIV

Louisiana at Its Best! Recipes

Cajun Cooking & Shrimp Mistakes

Just because you live in Louisiana doesn't mean you automatically know how to cook Cajun food. Phil and I were both raised in north Louisiana, and Cajun cooking is a south Louisiana delicacy. But it didn't take us long to figure out that the Cajuns had some secrets we wanted to know about.

We didn't, and still don't, eat out much, but when we would go to a restaurant that served Cajun food, we would pick that dish apart, looking to duplicate the recipe. One way I've always figured out a dish was with my nose. That's right—I just smell it. Well, I guess I had gone too far at one restaurant when I looked up to see a surprised waiter looking at my nose covered in crawfish étouffée! Phil just looked the other way like he didn't know me.

But this story ends well, as we were later asked to eat at NOLA, a restaurant in New Orleans owned by the famous chef Emeril Lagasse. To my delight, we were invited to see the kitchen and watch the chef prepare the meal. I can assure you—I kept my nose away from the pot!

Phil and I have shared the journey of learning new recipes and growing together as cooks. Every couple should have at least one thing they cherish together. Through cooking, Phil and I have grown to appreciate each other's gifts and to value each

Above: This picture really looks like the "best of Louisiana." I love it! Sadie with her Papaw Phil and Uncle Si enjoying one of the many rivers we fish on in northeast Louisiana.

other's opinion. That will go a long way in keeping a marriage healthy. Speaking of valuing each other's gifts, I have another story for you.

Many years ago, my good friend Sherry and I decided to fry shrimp. I made the batter out of flour, eggs, and milk. It looked a little thick, but we figured it would be okay, so we started dipping the shrimp and throwing them in the hot oil. Shrimp have a distinctive shape—sort of like a comma, with a big top and small tail. But as Sherry and I spooned out the first few shrimp, they just looked like little balls of flour. The distinctive shrimp shape was nowhere to be found. But we kept on frying and eventually had a platter full, and we served them up with homemade french fries and salad. We waited for our hungry husbands to heap compliments on our efforts. Phil took one bite and declared there was no shrimp in his bite at all! Somehow we had managed to fry a few pieces of the

thick batter without a shrimp being involved at all! From that day forward, Phil has been the shrimp fryer in our family. It's fine with me—trust me, there's plenty for me to do in the kitchen and Phil's shrimp are the best!

Don't be afraid to admit your husband is better than you at some things. Hey—sit back and let him enjoy being the best! God made us all valuable!

*Top: This picture was taken in the early 1980s by the Ouachita River. I'm sure we had a feast with this big fish! The little boy is Marshall Flowers, a friend of our family's. **Above:** Jase is showing Lily the fine art of peeling a crawfish. We teach them young so we don't have to peel them for the kids. Every man for himself when it comes to eating crawfish!*

Crawfish Balls

Makes 8 to 10 servings • Large cast-iron skillet • Deep heavy pot • Deep-fry thermometer

⅔ cup olive oil

2 large white or red onions, finely chopped

1 celery stalk, finely chopped

1 bell pepper, finely chopped

2 teaspoons finely chopped parsley

6 garlic cloves, finely chopped

Salt and black pepper

2 pounds crawfish tail meat, cut into small pieces

4 cups bread crumbs (crush dried bread in your hands or use store-bought unseasoned crumbs)

2 large eggs

Peanut oil, for frying

Duck Commander Cajun Seasoning (mild or zesty) or other Cajun seasoning

1. In a large skillet, heat the olive oil over medium heat. Add the onions, celery, bell pepper, parsley, and garlic, season with salt and pepper, and cook until soft, about 10 minutes.

2. Turn off the heat and add the crawfish, 3 cups of the bread crumbs, and the eggs and mix well.

3. Shape into golf-ball-size balls, or you can form it into patties.

4. Fill the pot about halfway with peanut oil and heat on medium heat to about 350°F (don't get your oil too hot).

5. Roll the crawfish balls/patties in the remaining bread crumbs. Fry a few at a time for 4 to 5 minutes, until golden brown. Drain on paper towels, and while still hot, sprinkle with the Cajun seasoning.

A Note from Miss Kay

It makes me happy, happy, happy that I married a man who loves to cook. This is one of the many recipes that Phil makes while I'm busy doing some other dish. Crawfish Balls make a great appetizer, but they will disappear fast!

Just Right White Rice

1 cup rice makes 2 servings • Saucepan with a lid

1 cup long-grain white rice (see Tip)
2 cups water
1 teaspoon salt

Bring the rice, water, and salt to a boil on medium-high heat. Let the water boil down to almost level with the rice, then put the lid on it and turn the heat down to the lowest setting. Allow to steam for 20 minutes.

Tip For every cup of rice you use, you will use twice that amount of water. So whatever the amount of rice you want to cook, just use twice that amount of water. Figure ½ cup of raw rice per person, so 1 cup of uncooked rice will feed two people.

A Note from Phil
Some of the best dishes are served with rice—Jambalaya (page 119), Étouffée (page 116), Pinto Beans & Sausage (page 16), and even Corn Shrimp Soup (page 91). Getting your rice right makes all the difference!

Phil's Sauce Piquante

Makes 12 servings • Dutch oven

1 cup peanut oil
1 cup all-purpose flour
1 cup diced onion
1 cup diced celery
1 cup diced green bell pepper
½ cup chopped green onions or
  scallions
10 garlic cloves, minced
4 pounds meat of your choice, cut in
  1½-inch chunks (deer or duck or
  seafood)
2 cans (14.5 ounces each) stewed
  tomatoes
1 can (6 ounces) tomato paste
1 can (14.75 ounces) chicken broth,
  plus more if needed
3 bay leaves
Dash of hot sauce (your choice)
Pinch of dried basil
Salt and black pepper
½ cup chopped fresh parsley
Just Right White Rice (page 110), for
  serving

1. In a Dutch oven, heat the oil over medium heat. Add the flour and cook, stirring constantly, until the roux is the color of a Hershey bar. (If you heat the oil first on medium heat to just short of smoking, then whisk in the flour, the roux will be ready quicker.) This should take about 20 minutes.

2. Add the onion, celery, bell pepper, green onion, and garlic to the roux and cook, stirring constantly, until the vegetables are well coated and starting to soften, about 5 minutes. Be careful not to let anything burn.

3. Stir the meat slowly into the roux and vegetables. If you are using seafood, don't add it yet.

4. Stir in the tomatoes, tomato paste, chicken broth, bay leaves, hot sauce, basil, salt, and pepper. Cook for 2 hours to 2 hours and 30 minutes if you added the meat, 1 hour if not, and add the seafood in the last 15 minutes. (Shrimp, crab meat, and crawfish cook quickly.)

5. Add the parsley. It should now look like a thick gravy. Add more broth if needed.

6. Remove the bay leaves before serving over rice.

A Note from Phil

Sauce Piquante is always served over rice. Remember: seafood cooks quickly, so don't add it too early. You can really use this sauce with any type of meat. Check out the recipe opposite to guarantee that you get your rice "just right."

Jay's Duck Wraps

Makes 8 to 12 servings • Outdoor grill

8 to 12 duck breasts

1 package (8 ounces) cream cheese, softened

8 to 12 jalapeño slices (either from a jar or sliced fresh)

1 package (5 ounces) Duck Commander Seasoning Rub

8 to 12 thin slices of bacon

Honey (any kind will work)

1. Soak the duck breasts in salted water overnight in the refrigerator.

2. Heat the grill to medium.

3. Cut an incision down the length of each breast, along the side, without cutting through to the other side. Stuff each breast with cream cheese and one jalapeño slice. Coat each breast with the seasoning rub and wrap with one slice of bacon. Secure with toothpicks.

4. Cook on the open grill until the bacon is crisp and the cream cheese starts to ooze out. It's okay for duck to be medium-rare.

5. Drizzle honey over each breast and cook an additional 1 to 2 minutes to glaze. Remove the toothpicks before serving.

A Note from Miss Kay

We love adding new cooks to our family. My granddaughter Anna is a blessed wife to have a husband who loves to grill. Jay loves to cook and often grills or barbecues for our whole family.

Mustard-Fried Crappie (We Call Them Perch)

Large deep cast-iron skillet • Deep-fry thermometer

Crappie (any number you or your
  fisherman have caught)
Salt and black pepper
Yellow mustard
All-purpose flour
Peanut oil, for frying
Duck Commander Cajun Seasoning
  (mild or zesty)

1. Fillet your crappie. This means to take the meat of the fish away from the bones, using a sharp knife. If you have never done this and don't have a grandpa around to show you how, there are several YouTube videos with instructions. I've never see them, but my kids tell me this is true.

2. Sprinkle the filleted fish with salt and pepper. Coat the fish with mustard, and roll in flour (about 1 tablespoon mustard and 3 tablespoons flour for each fillet).

3. Fill the skillet about halfway with peanut oil and heat on medium heat to about 350°F (don't get your oil too hot).

4. Fry a few fillets at a time until golden brown; this will only take a few minutes. Drain on paper towels, and while still hot, sprinkle with Cajun seasoning.

A Note from Miss Kay
In Louisiana, we love our fish, and preparing it can be a competitive activity. Fresh from the river and piping hot is the best way to serve fish!

Fried Crawfish Tails

Makes 6 servings • Large deep cast-iron skillet • Deep-fry thermometer

2 pounds crawfish tail meat (thawed if frozen)

Salt and black pepper

Duck Commander Cajun Seasoning (mild or zesty)

3 large eggs, beaten

2 cups all-purpose flour

Vegetable oil, for frying

1. Season the crawfish with salt, pepper, and Cajun seasoning. Dip the crawfish in the eggs (this is called an egg wash) then roll them in flour (this will keep the tails from sticking to each other when cooking).

2. Fill the skillet about halfway with oil and heat the oil to 350°F over medium-high heat. Add the crawfish tails a handful at a time and cook until golden brown and just done, about 1 minute. Drain on paper towels and eat quickly.

A Note from Miss Kay

Crawfish dishes are practically their own food group in Louisiana. We boil, fry, steam, bake, add them to other dishes, or serve it alone. But any way we serve it, it gets eaten!

Easy Crawfish Étouffée

Makes 4 servings • Large skillet

1 stick (¼ pound) butter
2 white onions, diced
2 celery stalks, diced
1 bell pepper, diced
5 garlic cloves, finely chopped
1 can (10.75 ounces) cream of
    mushroom soup
1 soup can of water
1 to 1½ pounds crawfish tail meat,
    fresh or frozen
½ teaspoon Duck Commander Cajun
    Seasoning (mild or zesty)
Salt and black pepper
Garlic powder
1 tablespoon chopped parsley
Just Right White Rice (page 110), for
    serving

1. In the skillet, melt the butter over medium-low heat. Add the onions, celery, bell pepper, and garlic, and cook, stirring occasionally, until they are soft, about 8 minutes.

2. Stir in the soup and water, bring to a boil, and boil for 2 to 3 minutes to reduce slightly. Add the crawfish, Cajun seasoning, and salt, pepper, and garlic powder to taste. Simmer for 10 to 15 minutes, to heat the crawfish through. Stir in the parsley and serve over rice.

A Note from Miss Kay

Étouffée is a dish found in Cajun and creole cooking. Most people think it's hard to make, but Phil made this version up, and it's so easy to make and delicious to eat. Étouffée is thicker than soup and is served over rice. This is a small-family version, so double or triple everything for a larger family.

Phil's Crawfish Fettuccine

Makes 10 to 12 servings • Large pot • Dutch oven

2 packages (1 pound each) fettuccine
pasta

2 sticks (½ pound) butter

1 bell pepper, chopped

3 celery stalks, chopped

2 large white onions, chopped

6 garlic cloves, finely chopped

2 teaspoons black pepper

Pinch of Duck Commander Cajun
Seasoning (mild or zesty) or other
Cajun seasoning

2 tablespoons chopped fresh parsley

2 pounds crawfish tail meat (thawed
if frozen)

3 tablespoons all-purpose flour

1 can (10.75 ounces) cream of
mushroom soup, or 2 cans if you
want it wetter

½ pound Velveeta cheese, cut into
chunks

1½ cups sour cream

1 cup grated Parmesan cheese

Salt

1. In a large pot of boiling water, cook the pasta according to the package directions. Drain and set aside.

2. In the Dutch oven, melt the butter over medium heat. Add the bell pepper, celery, onions, and garlic and cook, stirring occasionally until the vegetables are soft, about 15 minutes.

3. Add the pepper, Cajun seasoning, and parsley. Add the crawfish and cook for 4 to 5 minutes.

4. Stir in the flour and cook for another minute.

5. Add the soup, Velveeta, sour cream, Parmesan cheese, the pasta, and salt to taste. Stir it all together and heat until everything is hot and the cheeses are melted.

A Note from Phil

Crawfish season isn't like deer or duck season. There's no laws about catching crawfish. But there are times when the crawfish are better, and in Louisiana that is usually from January to the middle of August. The peak months are March and April. Crawfish are easy to boil, but we usually just buy them already boiled. After everyone has eaten their share, we peel the ones that are left over and save them for dishes like étouffée and this fettuccine.

Phil's Jambalaya

Makes 10 to 12 servings • Large (7- to 8-quart) heavy-bottomed cooking pot with a lid • Heavy spatula

½ cup vegetable oil

1 chicken (3½ pounds), cut up in small pieces

¾ pound andouille sausage, sliced ¼ inch thick (we use Savoie's)

1 package (about 7 ounces) tasso, cut into ¼-inch slices (we use Savoie's)

2 bell peppers, diced

3 small celery stalks, diced

2 large white onions, diced

5 garlic cloves, finely chopped

1 can (28 ounces) stewed tomatoes

1 can (6 ounces) tomato paste

1 tablespoon chopped parsley

5 cups uncooked rice

8 cups chicken broth

Duck Commander Cajun Seasoning (mild or zesty)

Salt and black pepper

1. In the large pot, heat the oil on medium-high heat. Add the chicken, sausage, and tasso and cook until the chicken has browned, about 5 minutes per side.

2. Add the bell peppers, celery, onions, garlic, stewed tomatoes, tomato paste, and parsley. Bring to a simmer, cover, and cook for 45 minutes.

3. Add the rice, chicken broth, and Cajun seasoning, salt, and pepper to taste.

4. Cover and lower the heat to medium-low. With a heavy spatula (one that won't bend) roll the jambalaya from bottom to top every 3 minutes to keep the rice from sticking. Continue rolling the jambalaya for 30 minutes. Replace the lid each time.

5. After 30 minutes, remove from the heat. Let stand covered for 20 minutes before serving.

A Note from Phil

Many Louisiana dishes are served with rice, but jambalaya is the only one that includes rice in the cooking. The other dishes are poured over the rice. This is the perfect dish for a large crowd. It's filling and everyone seems to like it.

Hushpuppies

Makes about 36 hushpuppies • Deep-fryer or large heavy pot

2½ cups yellow cornmeal

½ cup all-purpose flour

4 teaspoons baking powder

1 teaspoon baking soda

1 teaspoon salt

2 teaspoons sugar

2 large eggs

1½ cups buttermilk

1 small white onion, finely chopped

¼ cup finely chopped jalapeño peppers (optional, but it's good this way)

1 quart peanut oil, for frying

1. In a large bowl, stir together the cornmeal, flour, baking powder, baking soda, salt, and sugar. In a separate bowl, beat together the eggs, buttermilk, onion, and jalapeño. Stir the wet ingredients into the dry ingredients.

2. Fill the deep-fryer with oil according to the manufacturer's directions, or fill a heavy pot about halfway. Heat the oil to 350°F (over medium-high heat for the pot). Check the oil temperature by dropping in a small chunk of bread. It should brown quickly.

3. Carefully drop in batter by rounded tablespoonfuls and cook until golden brown, 1 to 2 minutes. Drain on paper towels and serve hot.

A Note from Miss Kay

In Louisiana, hushpuppy recipes are about as common as cooks. They are almost always served with fried fish. They are either dropped by spoonfuls into hot grease or shaped in some way. Korie's grandmother uses a cookie squeeze to shape hers. Either way, the taste is the same—fantastic!

Granny's Bread Pudding with Rum Sauce

Makes 8 to 10 servings • Microwave • Microwave-safe bowl • 9 x 13-inch casserole dish (glass, if available) Medium saucepan

Pudding

½ stick (4 tablespoons) butter
1 loaf white or French bread (about 9 ounces), torn into 1- to 1½-inch pieces
3 large eggs
2 cups sugar
½ teaspoon salt
1 quart whole milk

Rum Sauce

1½ cups sugar
1½ sticks (12 tablespoons) butter, barely melted
1 can (14 ounces) sweetened condensed milk (I use Eagle Brand)
1 large egg yolk
2 teaspoons vanilla extract
½ teaspoon rum flavoring

1. Make the pudding: Melt the butter in a microwave-safe bowl (we love modern America!). Do not let it boil, just melt, and set it aside so it will not be too hot.

2. Place the bread in the casserole.

3. In a large mixing bowl, beat the eggs with a fork. Stir in the sugar and salt. Add the cooled melted butter and gradually stir in the milk. Pour this over the torn bread. Let stand for 30 to 45 minutes for the bread to absorb the liquid.

4. While the pudding is standing, heat the oven to 350°F.

5. Bake the pudding until risen, golden brown, and not runny, about 45 minutes.

6. Make the sauce: In a medium saucepan, off the heat, combine the sugar, melted butter, and condensed milk, stirring until well combined.

7. Put the pan on the stove and cook on medium-high heat until thick. Stir to keep it from sticking. If it starts to stick, turn down the heat to low or move the pan off the stove.

8. In a small bowl, beat the egg yolk. Add the warm sauce to the egg yolk, 1 tablespoon at a time, stirring as you add. You are trying to prevent the egg from cooking to a hard-boiled state.

9. Stir in the vanilla and rum flavoring.

10. Serve the sauce over each piece of bread pudding, or pour over the top of the entire pan of pudding.

A Note from Miss Kay

I have read that bread pudding dates back centuries. Its original purpose was to use stale bread, so nothing was wasted. It is baked worldwide in different ways. Louisianans love a good bread pudding. This recipe is easy to make and delicious. If you've never eaten bread pudding, today's a good day to start!

7.

Dinner on the Grounds

∿∿∿∿∿∿∿∿∿∿∿∿∿∿∿∿∿∿∿∿

One of the very nicest things about life is the way we must regularly stop whatever it is we are doing and devote our attention to eating.

—Luciano Pavarotti

Stay on good terms with each other, held together by love. Be ready with a meal or a bed when it's needed. Why, some have extended hospitality to angels without ever knowing it!

—Hebrews 13:2, *The Message*

Dinner on the Grounds Recipes

More than Enough

I would say there's not a child in the South who hasn't attended a dinner on the grounds. "Potluck" and "church picnic" are other names for that special occasion when your church declares it's time to get together in the parking lot or the yard next door for some fellowship. These special occasions are as much a part of southern living as church revivals, and many times these two events go hand in hand. Or perhaps the dinner will be held on special occasions like Easter or Mother's Day. In any case, it's always a good excuse for folks to get together.

The idea of dinner on the grounds is for each family to bring plenty of food for their own family and then enough to feed another family or two. I think the whole idea started in a day and time when Sunday afternoons were more leisurely and the idea of spreading a blanket on the ground and sharing a meal seemed like a great way to spend the day. In today's world, it's rare to find a group of people willing to eat on the ground, but you can still find people who enjoy great fellowship. Most churches today will put out tables, forgoing the "ground" part, but the "dinner" part is still brought and shared by each family.

I have always loved these special occasions because I love visiting with folks, and I love getting to taste the cooking of the ladies in our church. Macaroni and cheese, chicken spaghetti, and banana pudding are a few of the many dishes sure to show up at any dinner on the grounds gathering. For the last few years at our congregation, we

Above: I think I was five in this picture. Who knows, maybe we were on our way to dinner on the grounds.

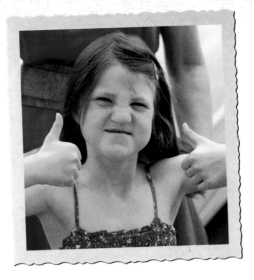

have held a Duck Commander Sunday service followed by a dinner on the grounds. Last year, so many people came that we wondered if we would have enough food. But we did. We shouldn't have doubted our church family. They are the best!

It's fun to watch the children eye all the choices of food, especially in this fast-food world we live in now. I'm sure there are many dishes at a dinner on the grounds they have never seen before. As a child, I can remember filling every square inch of my plate. The church I grew up in was very small, but the women could cook! My plate would get so full I could hardly carry it and my glass of lemonade. I would spot my mama saving a place for me and my sister, Ann. I can remember noticing that my mama didn't have a plate fixed for herself. I asked her where her plate was and she answered, "Oh, there will be plenty here for me to eat." Mama knew that my eyes were bigger than my stomach, and there was no need to waste food.

Yes, another life lesson was taught at dinner on the grounds: no matter how much you have, there's never enough to waste. Mama was right—my eyes were too big for my stomach and she had plenty to eat. 🦆

*Above: Mia gives a thumbs-up as she walks over to join the fun after church one Sunday. **Opposite:** Jep gathers up two of his kids and heads over to the dinner on the grounds after church. I'm wondering where his food contribution is. I guess he figured I would make enough for all of us.*

Spoon Butter Rolls

Makes 1 dozen rolls • Regular 12-cup muffin tin

Nonstick cooking spray

1 envelope (¼ ounce) active dry yeast

2 cups very warm water (105° to 110°F)

1 stick (¼ pound) butter

¼ cup sugar

1 large egg

4 cups self-rising flour

1. Heat the oven to 400°F. Lightly grease the muffin tin cups with cooking spray.

2. Sprinkle the yeast over the warm water. Let stand until foamy, about 5 minutes.

3. In a large mixing bowl, beat the butter and sugar until well combined and creamy. Beat in the egg.

4. Add the yeast to the butter mixture. Add the flour and stir until well combined.

5. Drop by spoonfuls into the muffin cups. Bake until browned, 20 to 25 minutes. Cool in the pan or eat while still hot.

A Note from Miss Kay

This dough will keep in a tightly sealed container in the refrigerator for several days. Be sure to use self-rising flour so you'll have nice fluffy rolls.

Roast Beef & Vegetable Soup

Makes 8 to 10 servings • Large (7- to 8-quart) cooking pot with a lid

1 boneless chuck roast (2 to 3 pounds, depending on family size), cut into 1-inch chunks

1½ teaspoons garlic powder

Duck Commander Cajun Seasoning (mild or zesty) or other Cajun seasoning

1 bay leaf

Salt and black pepper

6 red or white potatoes, peeled and cut into 1-inch chunks

6 carrots, peeled and sliced 1 inch thick

1 large onion, chopped

1 large bell pepper, chopped

2 celery stalks, chopped

2 garlic cloves, chopped

1 can (28 ounces) stewed or diced tomatoes

1 can (12 ounces) tomato paste

1. Place meat in the pot with water to cover and bring to a boil over medium-high heat. Skim any foam that rises to the surface.

2. Add the garlic powder, Cajun seasoning (apply liberally), bay leaf, and salt and pepper to taste, reduce to a simmer, and cook 1 hour.

3. Add the potatoes, carrots, onion, bell pepper, celery, garlic, stewed tomatoes, and tomato paste and return to a boil. Reduce to a simmer, cover, and cook 1 hour longer or until the meat and vegetables are tender. Remove the bay leaf before serving.

A Note from Miss Kay

There's nothing like a pot of soup cooking in the kitchen on a chilly day! You can make this for lunch, and it will roll right over to supper time. It's best with a big slice of cornbread and a houseful of family!

Squash Casserole

Makes 6 to 8 servings • Large pot • Large skillet • 9x13-inch casserole dish

¾ stick (6 tablespoons) butter, plus
    more for the casserole
7 medium yellow squash (about 2¼
    pounds), cut in half lengthwise and
    sliced ½ inch thick
1 medium onion, chopped
1 medium bell pepper, chopped
1 can (14.75 ounces) cream-style corn
1 large egg, lightly beaten
Salt and black pepper
1 sleeve Ritz crackers, crumbled

1. Heat the oven to 350°F. Lightly butter the casserole.

2. In a large pot of boiling water, cook the squash until tender, about 5 minutes. Drain well. Transfer to a large mixing bowl.

3. In a large skillet, melt the butter over medium heat. Add the onion and bell pepper and cook, stirring occasionally, until tender, about 7 minutes.

4. Add the onion mixture, creamed corn, and egg to the squash and mix well to combine. Add salt and pepper to taste. Pour into the casserole and scatter the cracker crumbs over the top.

5. Bake until set, about 1 hour.

A Note from Miss Kay
Squash isn't something the kids will run for, but the adults will. This is a great summer dish and really brightens a table.

Lasagna

Makes 8 servings • Large pot • Large skillet •9x13-inch casserole dish

1 pound hamburger meat

1 jar (28 ounces) spaghetti sauce

1½ cups water

1 container (15 ounces) ricotta cheese

2 cups shredded mozzarella cheese
    (8 ounces)

¾ cup grated Parmesan cheese

2 large eggs

¼ cup chopped parsley

½ teaspoon salt

¼ teaspoon black pepper

1 package (8 ounces) lasagna noodles

2 cups shredded cheddar cheese
    (8 ounces)

1. Heat the oven to 350°F.

2. In a large skillet, cook the meat over medium heat, breaking it up with a spoon, until no longer pink, about 5 minutes. Drain any fat from the pan.

3. Add the spaghetti sauce and water to the meat, bring to a boil, reduce to a simmer, and cook 10 minutes, until thickened.

4. In a medium bowl, stir together the ricotta, 1 cup of the mozzarella, ½ cup of the Parmesan, the eggs, parsley, salt, and pepper.

5. Pour about 1 cup of the sauce on the bottom of the casserole. Arrange a layer of uncooked noodles on top of the sauce. Add just enough sauce to cover the noodles, then top with ⅓ of the ricotta mixture. Sprinkle with ⅔ cup of the cheddar and ⅓ cup of the remaining mozzarella.

6. Repeat until you've made 3 layers. Finish off the top with the remaining cheddar, mozzarella, and Parmesan cheeses.

7. Cover with foil and bake for 45 minutes. Uncover and bake 15 minutes longer or until the top is golden brown. Let stand 10 minutes before cutting into pieces.

A Note from Lisa

Lasagna is always a great dish to feed lots of people. You might want to invest in an insulated bag to take your dishes to the church potluck. That way your food stays warm and everyone is Happy, Happy, Happy!

Sweet Potato Casserole

Makes 10 to 12 servings • 9x13-inch casserole dish

Pastry blender (Just Google "pastry blender" and see what they look like, then buy one at any store.)

Sweet Potatoes

Softened butter, for the casserole

3 cups mashed sweet potatoes (one 29-ounce can and one 16-ounce can, drained), or 2 pounds fresh sweet potatoes, baked or peeled and boiled, then mashed

1 cup granulated sugar

1 stick (¼ pound) butter, melted

2 large eggs

½ cup evaporated milk (I use Pet)

1 teaspoon ground cinnamon

1 teaspoon vanilla extract

Topping (here's the good part)

1½ cups packed brown sugar (either light or dark is okay)

⅔ cup self-rising flour

1½ sticks (12 tablespoons) cold butter, cut into bits

1½ cups coarsely chopped pecans

1. Heat the oven to 350°F. Lightly butter the casserole.

2. Make the sweet potatoes: In a large bowl, combine the mashed sweet potatoes, granulated sugar, butter, eggs, milk, cinnamon, and vanilla. Spoon into the casserole.

3. Make the topping: In a large bowl, combine the brown sugar and flour. With a pastry blender, cut in the butter and pecans. Scatter the topping over the sweet potatoes.

4. Bake at 350°F until the topping is crisp and the potatoes are piping hot, about 1 hour.

A Note from Miss Kay

This is a recipe my good friend and the great cook Luanne Watts makes. I think our entire church has gotten this recipe from her because it's so good. It's great for Thanksgiving or Easter or any time you want it! Thanks, Luanne, for sharing!

Chrys's Potato Casserole

Makes 12 to 15 servings • 9x13-inch casserole dish

1 stick (¼ pound) butter, melted

1 can (10.75 ounces) cream of mushroom soup

2 cups sour cream

2 tablespoons sliced green onion or scallion

4 cups shredded cheddar cheese (1 pound)

1 large bag (2 pounds) frozen hash browns (shredded or cubed), thawed

1 teaspoon salt

½ cup chopped cooked bacon (store-bought bacon bits are okay)

1. In a large bowl, mix together the butter, soup, sour cream, green onion, and 2 cups of the cheese. Stir in the hash browns and salt and spread the mixture in the casserole. Sprinkle the top with the remaining 2 cups of cheese and the bacon bits.

2. Cover with foil and bake for 1 hour and 15 minutes. Uncover and bake 15 minutes more or until the top is golden brown and crispy.

Tip Chrys says she melts her butter in the microwave first and uses the same bowl to mix in.

A Note from Miss Kay

This recipe is from Korie's mom, Chrys, who isn't known for her cooking, but with eleven grandkids I know she does cook. One of her best dishes is this potato casserole. It's perfect for company or a potluck. If you need to, double the recipe. Trust me, it will all be eaten.

Chocolate Sheet Cake

Makes 1 (9x13-inch) cake • 9x13-inch cake pan • Wax paper • Medium saucepan
Nonstick cooking spray, for the cake pan

Cake

2 cups all-purpose flour, sifted

2 cups granulated sugar

1½ teaspoons salt

2 large eggs

1 teaspoon baking soda

½ cup buttermilk or sour cream

1 teaspoon vanilla extract

3 tablespoons unsweetened cocoa
   powder

1 stick (¼ pound) butter

½ cup shortening

1 cup water

Icing

1 stick (¼ pound) butter

6 tablespoons evaporated milk (I use
   Pet)

1 tablespoon whole milk

1 package (16 ounces) powdered
   sugar

3 tablespoons unsweetened cocoa
   powder

1 teaspoon vanilla extract

1½ cups chopped pecans

1. Heat the oven to 350°F. Grease the cake pan with cooking spray and line the bottom with wax paper; grease the paper.

2. Make the cake: In a large bowl, sift together the flour, sugar, and salt; set aside.

3. In a small bowl, beat the eggs, then stir in the baking soda, buttermilk, and vanilla.

4. Put the cocoa powder in the saucepan, add the butter and shortening, and melt over medium heat. Whisk in the water, bring to a boil, and pour over the flour mixture. Add the egg mixture and mix thoroughly by hand.

5. Pour the batter into the pan. Bake until the cake starts to pull away at the sides and a toothpick inserted in the center comes out clean, 20 to 25 minutes.

6. Let the cake cool in the pan on a wire rack. Run a spatula around the sides and invert the cake onto a serving platter.

7. While the cake is cooling, make the icing: In a medium saucepan over low heat, melt the butter with both milks (do not boil). Remove from the heat and beat in the sugar, cocoa powder, and vanilla. Stir in the pecans until well mixed. Spread over the cake immediately.

A Note from Miss Kay

This cake is perfect for a crowd. It's made in a large sheet cake pan and is only one layer, so it serves lots of folks. I usually make this and something that isn't chocolate to give guests a choice, but most of the time they just take some of each.

Banana Pudding

Makes 8 servings • Double boiler • 9 x 13-inch casserole dish or large glass bowl

2 sticks (½ pound) butter, melted

2 cups sugar

⅔ cup all-purpose flour

1 teaspoon salt

1 can (12 ounces) evaporated milk
(I use Pet)

¾ cup whole milk

6 large egg yolks

1 teaspoon vanilla extract

40 vanilla wafer cookies

3 bananas

Lemon juice

Whipped topping (optional)

1. In the top of a double boiler over simmering water, melt the butter. Whisk in the sugar, flour, and salt. Add the milks and stir continuously until the mixture thickens. This may take 30 to 40 minutes.

2. Once it's thickened, stir a little into the egg yolks. This will temper the yolks and keep them from cooking too fast. Stir the tempered egg yolks into the mixture in the double boiler and cook, stirring, until when you pull out the spoon, the mixture does not drip.

3. Remove the top from the double boiler. Stir in the vanilla.

4. Spread a little of the pudding in the bottom of the casserole. Top with the vanilla wafers. Slice the bananas in rounds, dip them lightly in lemon juice to preserve their freshness, and place on the wafers. Pour the remaining pudding on top. If you like, add more vanilla wafers to the top of the pudding and add spoonfuls of whipped topping.

5. To be really fancy, layer the pudding, bananas, and vanilla wafers in nice drinking glasses and add a little whipped topping.

A Note from Miss Kay

I guess if I'm famous for any of my dishes, this would be it. At almost every church gathering, I'm asked to bring banana pudding. I do love it myself, so I never mind making it.

Everybody's Favorite Crunch Salad

Makes 4 to 6 servings

Dressing

¼ cup packed brown sugar (either light or dark is okay)

2 teaspoons salt

6 tablespoons seasoned rice vinegar (this is rice vinegar with salt and pepper already added)

½ cup vegetable oil

4 drops Tabasco sauce (if you like more bite, add 2 more drops)

Salad

1½ cups crispy chow mein noodles

¾ cup hulled sunflower seeds

½ cup slivered almonds, toasted

1 head romaine lettuce or curly leaf lettuce, cut into bite-size pieces, washed, dried well, and chilled

4 green onions or scallions, thinly sliced

1. Make the dressing: In a small jar or plastic container with a lid, combine the brown sugar, salt, vinegar, oil, and Tabasco and shake well to combine; set aside.

2. Make the salad: In a small bowl, combine the chow mein noodles, sunflower seeds, and almonds.

3. Just before serving, layer the lettuce, green onions, and noodle mix in a bowl.

4. Pour dressing over the salad (give it a couple of shakes if it's separated) and mix well. Serve immediately.

A Note from Miss Kay

As salads go, this is one of the best. We have a mentoring program at our church called Heart to Home where our younger women meet with the older women once a month. This salad is always a favorite. There's just something about toasted almonds that makes everything taste better. If you start taking this salad to your church or family gatherings, be ready, because you'll be asked to bring it again.

Best Brisket Ever

Makes about 15 servings • Roasting pan • Medium saucepan • Outdoor grill (optional)

1 beef brisket (10 pounds)

1 stick (¼ pound) butter

1 medium onion, chopped

1 bottle (14 ounces) catsup (1⅔ cups)

½ cup packed brown sugar (either light or dark is okay)

2 tablespoons white vinegar

2 tablespoons lemon juice

1½ teaspoon salt

½ teaspoon black pepper

½ teaspoon cayenne pepper

Dash of Louisiana hot sauce or Tabasco sauce (as much as you like)

1. Heat the oven to 250°F.

2. Wrap the brisket in a double layer foil. Place in the roasting pan and bake for 3 hours and 30 minutes to 4 hours or until tender enough to be pierced with a knife.

3. Meanwhile, in a medium saucepan, melt the butter over medium heat. Add the onion and cook, stirring occasionally, until soft, about 7 minutes. Add the catsup, sugar, vinegar, lemon juice, salt, pepper, cayenne, and hot sauce to taste. Mix well and set aside.

4. When the brisket is tender, carefully remove it from the foil (the juices will be hot). Discard all grease. If you have one, heat the grill to 350°F. If not, turn on the oven broiler.

5. Brush the sauce on the brisket. Put on the grill for 20 minutes on each side. If you don't have an outdoor grill, put the brisket back in the oven without the foil and broil for 5 minutes. Turn the brisket over and broil 5 to 10 minutes longer, or until the sauce is bubbly and lightly caramelized.

A Note from Miss Kay

Brisket is a tougher cut of meat, so you need to cook it slowly. This will make it moist and easy to eat. In the South, brisket is usually served with barbecue sauce or rubbed with special seasonings, as in this recipe. It's great for a crowd.

Stuffed Bell Peppers

Makes 6 servings • Large pot • 9 x 13-inch casserole dish

6 large bell peppers

2 pounds ground meat (beef, pork, or turkey, or a mix will work, but I use beef)

1 medium onion, chopped

1 celery stalk, chopped

3 garlic cloves, finely chopped

1 large egg

1 can (12 ounces) tomato paste

1 teaspoon salt

1 can (8 ounces) tomato sauce

1. Heat the oven to 375°F.

2. Slice the tops off the bell peppers, cut out the stems, and coarsely chop the tops (these will be part of the stuffing). Remove the seeds and ribs from inside the peppers.

3. In a large pot of boiling water, cook the peppers for 5 minutes to soften. Turn upside down to drain and cool.

4. In a large bowl, combine the meat, chopped pepper tops, onion, celery, garlic, egg, tomato paste, and salt. Stuff the meat mixture into the bell pepper shells, place them standing up in the casserole, and top each with some tomato sauce. Bake until the filling is firm and the peppers are piping hot, about 45 minutes.

A Note from Miss Kay

If you like meatloaf, you will love stuffed bell peppers, because the peppers are stuffed with my meatloaf recipe. Also, if you love a meal with a "presentation," this is for you. It looks great and tastes great!

8.

Miss Kay's "Muffins & Mentoring" Group

〰〰〰〰〰〰〰〰〰〰〰〰〰〰〰

All happiness depends on

a leisurely breakfast.

—John Gunther

Guide older women into lives of reverence so they end up as neither gossips nor drunks, but models of goodness. By looking at them, the younger women will know how to love their husbands and children, be virtuous and pure, keep a good house, be good wives. We don't want anyone looking down on God's Message because of their behavior.

—Titus 2:4–5, *The Message*

Recipes Perfect for a Mentoring Group

〰〰〰〰〰〰ᐯᐯᐯᐯᐯᐯᐯᐯᐯᐯᐯᐯᐯᐯᐯᐯ〰〰〰〰〰〰

"Muffins for Moms" Mentoring Group

Muffins for Moms" wasn't my idea, but I was quickly pulled into it by two of my good friends, Kim Neal and Darlene Nugent. I didn't mind it, though, because it involves two things I love—cooking and talking. I've spent most of my adult years talking to young women about their marriages and encouraging them to stay strong and be the women God wants them to be. "Muffins for Moms" is a mentoring group that meets once a week. We meet in the mornings, so we bring some type of breakfast food. But this is just one of the mentoring groups I've been involved in over the years. Another one I am involved in now meets once a

month for a meal. Through these groups, I get to share my life story and hear the life stories of other women.

Part of what I always tell the young women I encounter is about my early years of marriage when Phil wasn't living right. Phil had graduated from Louisiana Tech University and had already begun a life of partying. Phil graduated with a master's in English and had landed a real job

Above: Each week one of our group members hosts our session. We learned a long time ago that it's not about the place, it's about the people. I'm thankful for each of these women and their desire to grow to become better women.

at a school in Junction City, Arkansas, so I had hopes that his life would turn around. But I soon discovered our "smooth sailing years" would have to wait. Phil chose to hunt and party over being a husband and a parent. His partying lifestyle got so bad that I thought our marriage was over, and if it wasn't for hearing my Nanny's voice in my head telling me, "One day you will have to fight for your marriage," I might have gone the route of divorce. But I didn't, and in time and with lots of prayer, Phil turned his life around and we began a new life living for Jesus.

Our former youth minister, Mike Kellett, used to tell our young people, "When you're through with sin, it's not through with you." Meaning, once we turned our lives around and knew God had totally forgiven us, we still had to live with the consequences of our past mistakes. Our children had seen and heard things they did not need to see and hear at young ages. And Phil had to answer to the law for some of his crazy antics. But we plugged away at doing the right thing, and over time we made great progress, and our family grew strong in the Lord. As our children got older, we went through what many other parents go through—two of our boys began living a

*Above: Three of my boys went to a school of preaching, and Phil has preached for years; but I'm really the talker in the family, so teaching other women comes naturally to me. I love sharing my life with them and listening to them as they share theirs. **Opposite**: We can't resist a little silliness! Life is hard, and learning to laugh and have joy is a key part of getting through each day. Each of these women has a story. You do too. Share it with someone else and bless their day!*

life contrary to our beliefs. My heart was so heavy as I prayed and cried for my sons to get their lives right. Once again my prayers were answered, and today all my boys walk in the love of God. But the journey wasn't easy.

I'm so blessed to be able to tell my story and use it to help others who are struggling, whether it's in marriage and with their kids or whatever. God has given all of us life stories and, through those stories, healing can happen. The famous preacher Rick Warren says, "Never waste your hurts." I also believe that. I want my hurts to help heal others. You can do that, too!

I love all the women in this special group and thank God that I've been chosen to share my life with them. Wherever you are, look for someone in your life who needs a helping hand or a calming voice.

Good Morning Muffins

Makes 18 muffins • 2 regular 12-cup muffin tins

Nonstick cooking spray
2 large eggs
¾ cup vegetable oil
¼ cup milk
2 teaspoons vanilla extract
2 cups all-purpose flour
1 cup packed brown sugar (either
    light or dark is okay)
2 teaspoons baking soda
2 teaspoons ground cinnamon
½ teaspoon salt
1½ cups peeled and shredded apple
    (about 2 apples)
1 cup shredded carrots (1 large or 2
    medium)
½ cup sweetened shredded coconut
½ cup raisins
¾ cup sliced almonds

1. Heat the oven to 350°F. Lightly grease 18 of the muffin cups with cooking spray.

2. In a large bowl, whisk together the eggs, oil, milk, and vanilla until well combined. Add the flour, sugar, baking soda, cinnamon, and salt; stir just until dry ingredients are moistened.

3. Stir in the apples, carrots, coconut, raisins, and ½ cup of the almonds. Divide batter evenly among the greased muffin cups, filling each about ¾ full. Sprinkle the remaining almonds over the batter.

4. Bake 20 to 25 minutes, until a toothpick inserted in the center of a muffin comes out clean. Remove the muffins from the tins and cool on a wire rack.

   Tip You can use an ice cream scoop to easily scoop the batter into the muffin tins. Also, these can be wrapped and frozen for up to a couple of months.

A Note from Miss Kay

One of my sweet "muffin" ladies contributed this recipe. I always feel like I'm eating something really healthy with these muffins. Of course you can adjust it as you like. Some people don't like raisins, so feel free to leave them out. Enjoy!

Perfect Pumpkin Spread

Makes about 3 cups

1 package (8 ounces) cream cheese, softened

7 tablespoons pumpkin butter

1 cup chopped pecans

3 slices bacon, cooked, cooled, and crumbled (about 3 tablespoons)

About ½ cup chopped green onions or scallions

Crackers, for serving

Mix everything together. Serve with crackers of your choice.

A Note from Miss Kay

Our oldest son, Alan, was the preacher at our church for more than twenty years, so you know we've been a part of many showers and weddings. Our house is quite a distance from town, and sometimes I just have to stop at the store on my way to an event. This dip is perfect for those rushed times. I can mix it up right at the shower.

Peppery Good Dip

Makes about 4 cups

1 package (8 ounces) cream cheese, softened

1 cup mayonnaise or salad dressing

1 cup thinly sliced green onions or scallions

1 cup coarsely chopped pecans

1 cup shredded medium-sharp cheddar cheese

Small jar of hot pepper jelly, chilled

Crackers, for serving

1. Mix together all the ingredients except the pepper jelly and crackers. Spread evenly in a container or on a pretty serving plate. Chill, if time allows.

2. Spread chilled hot pepper jelly on top when you're ready to serve.

3. Serve with crackers of your choice. Ritz or Triscuit Thin Crisps work well.

Aunt Judy's Cranberry Salad

Makes 8 to 10 servings • Food processor (optional)

1 bag (12 ounces) fresh or frozen cranberries (about 3 cups), rinsed and dried

1 cup sugar

1 can (20 ounces) crushed pineapple, drained

2 cups miniature marshmallows

1 container (16 ounces) whipped topping (I use Cool Whip)

1 cup chopped pecans

1. In a food processor, pulse the cranberries and sugar together until coarsely chopped. Transfer to a container with a cover and refrigerate overnight. (If you don't have a processor, use a mallet or fork to crush the cranberries.)

2. The next morning, put the cranberries in a colander and drain off the juice. Transfer the cranberries to a large mixing or serving bowl and add the pineapple, marshmallows, whipped topping, and pecans and mix well. Refrigerate until you're ready to serve.

A Note from Miss Kay

Judy was Phil's older sister. She loved to cook and used it as a way to relax. She was an administrative nurse, which meant her job was very demanding. She was a great example to me when we first married and we constantly talked about cooking. She passed away in 2006 and is greatly missed.

Heavenly Made Muffins

Makes 1 dozen muffins • Regular 12-cup muffin tin

Nonstick cooking spray

2 cups sifted all-purpose flour

1 tablespoon baking powder

2 teaspoons sugar

½ teaspoon salt

1 large egg

1 cup milk

¼ cup vegetable oil, or vegetable shortening, melted

1. Heat the oven to 425°F. Lightly grease the muffin cups with cooking spray.

2. In a large mixing bowl, sift together the flour, baking powder, sugar, and salt. In a separate bowl, beat the egg until frothy. Add the milk and oil; mix well.

3. Make a well in the center of the flour. Pour in the milk mixture all at once. Stir quickly and lightly until just mixed, but some lumps can remain.

4. Quickly fill the muffin cups ⅔ full; wipe off any spilled drips of batter. (If the batter does not fill all of the cups, fill the empty ones with water to keep the grease from burning.)

5. Bake for 20 to 25 minutes, until a toothpick inserted in the center of a muffin comes out clean. Remove the muffins from the tins and serve warm, or cool on a wire rack.

A Note from Miss Kay

My mentoring group often meets in the mornings, so this muffin recipe is the perfect dish to bring and enjoy. It can easily be doubled for two muffin pans full. Also, you can use cute muffin liners for a happy morning treat.

Amazing Miniature Biscuits

Makes about 2½ to 3 dozen biscuits • Electric mixer • Cookie sheet • Rolling pin (optional)

2 sticks (½ pound) butter, softened

3 packages (8 ounces each) cream cheese, softened

3 cups self-rising flour, plus more for rolling (optional)

1. In a large bowl, with the electric mixer, beat the butter and cream cheese for 2 minutes until creamy and well combined. Gradually add the flour and beat on low speed until combined.

2. Quick shaping method: Drop by spoonfuls onto the ungreased cookie sheet.

3. A little longer method: Refrigerate the dough for 30 minutes. Transfer to a lightly floured counter and with a rolling pin, roll the dough to ½ inch thick. Cut with a miniature biscuit cutter and place on the ungreased cookie sheet.

4. Bake 15 to 17 minutes, until golden brown.

A Note from Miss Kay

I know I have three biscuit recipes in this book, but they're all delicious! And I love biscuits! This one came from my niece-in-law, Jil Dasher. They will literally melt in your mouth. Jil is a busy homeschooling mom of four, the daughter-in-law of Phil's sister Jan. She's also a great cook. I love that I am still learning from young cooks. I've discovered that there's always something to learn in the kitchen. That's what makes cooking so interesting.

Super Simple Sugar Cookies

Makes about 5 dozen cookies • Electric mixer • Cookie sheets • Wire cooling racks

4 cups all-purpose flour

1 teaspoon cream of tartar

½ teaspoon baking soda

¼ teaspoon salt

2 sticks (½ pound) butter, softened

1 cup vegetable oil

1 cup granulated sugar, plus more for dipping

1 cup powdered sugar

2 large eggs

1 teaspoon vanilla extract

1. In a medium bowl, stir together the flour, cream of tartar, baking soda, and salt. In a large bowl, with the electric mixer, beat the butter, oil, and both sugars until creamy. Add the eggs and vanilla, beating until well blended.

2. Gradually add the flour to the butter mixture, beating until well combined. The dough will be light and fluffy.

3. Drop by large spoonfuls onto cookie sheets, spacing the cookies about 2 inches apart.

4. Dip the bottom of a drinking glass in granulated sugar and press the cookies to ¼ inch thick.

5. Bake until the edges are golden brown, 8 to 10 minutes. Let cool on the sheets for a few minutes, then transfer to wire racks to cool completely.

A Note from Miss Kay

Slice-and-bake cookies have done away with the need for homemade cookie recipes, but I am still convinced these are way better. Plus, it's a great way for moms and children to connect. If you haven't done it in a while, spend some quality time cooking with your kiddos.

Phil's Famous Hot Cocoa

Makes 4 servings • Medium saucepan

⅓ cup unsweetened cocoa powder
½ cup sugar
Pinch of salt
⅓ cup hot water
1 quart milk
¾ teaspoon vanilla extract

1. In a medium saucepan, stir together the cocoa powder, sugar, and salt. Add the water, stirring to moisten the cocoa. Bring to a boil over medium heat. Boil, stirring constantly, for 2 minutes.

2. Add the milk, stir, and heat until just steaming (do not boil after adding the milk). Stir in the vanilla and serve.

A Note from Miss Kay
I know making homemade hot cocoa isn't necessary anymore with all the powdered mixes available, but it sure is good. If you're looking for a way to treat your friends, this will do the trick.

Creamy Green Grape Salad

Makes 6 to 8 servings • Large salad bowl

1 package (8 ounces) package cream
   cheese, softened
1 container (8 ounces) sour cream
½ cup granulated sugar
2 tablespoons brown sugar (either
   light or dark is okay)
1 teaspoon vanilla extract
1 large bunch (about 1½ pounds)
   seedless green grapes, washed,
   dried, and cut in half lengthwise
1 cup coarsely chopped pecans or
   walnuts

In the bowl, beat the cream cheese, sour cream, both sugars, and the vanilla until light and creamy. Add the grapes and stir until they are covered with the mixture. Sprinkle the pecans over the top, mix again, and refrigerate.

A Note from Miss Kay
This is such a simple dish, but it's a fun way to dress up grapes. Be sure to buy grapes that are firm to the touch and, when you shake them, are attached tightly to their stems.

Colorful Fruit Salad

Makes 12 servings • Large salad bowl

2 cans (20 ounces each) pineapple chunks, drained, half the juice saved

2 cans (11 ounces each) mandarin orange slices, drained

1 large bunch seedless green grapes, washed and dried

1 large bunch seedless red grapes, washed and dried

2 apples, cored and cut into small chunks

1 pint strawberries, washed, dried, hulled, and thickly sliced

1 can (21 ounces) peach pie filling

2 bananas

1. In a large salad bowl, stir together the pineapple, the reserved juice, and the orange slices. Stir in the green and red grapes, apples, and strawberries. The pineapple juice will keep the fruit fresh. (The salad can even be refrigerated and stored overnight.)

2. Stir in the pie filling.

3. At serving time, slice the bananas, add to the salad, and toss to coat with the juice. (The pineapple juice will keep the bananas fresh looking, too.)

A Note from Miss Kay

This recipe is one that Phil's sister Jan has shared with me. The pie filling at the end is optional. All the other fruit mixed together is great on its own if you don't have pie filling handy.

9.

Our Cajun Christmas

~~~~~~~~~~~~~~~~~~~~~~~~~~~

A recipe has no soul. You, as the cook,

must bring soul to the recipe.

—Thomas Keller

Instructed by the king, they set off. Then the star appeared again, the same star they had seen in the eastern skies. It led them on until it hovered over the place of the child. They could hardly contain themselves: They were in the right place! They had arrived at the right time!

—Matthew 2:9–10, *The Message*

Our Cajun Christmas Recipes

~~~~~~

Our Family Christmas

Christmas is my favorite time of year. I like to decorate every inch of my house, and yes, it's a good thing my house isn't that big or Phil might get a little nervous about my decorating obsession. This last year I had my niece Melissa come over to help me organize my decorations after Christmas, but they're still a mess. Her best efforts were no match for my decorations. Most of them are stored in a small house next door to our house that Alan and Lisa lived in when they were first married. The little granddaughters call it the "library" because I have so many books stored in there. They love to play in the "library," and any time we can't find them, we know where to look. Right now their playing space is crowded with my Christmas decorations. I'm sure it will stay that way until the next Christmas season, and I'll get Melissa to come help me again. The girls just walk around it all and act like there's not a big Santa staring at them all the time.

Many people have asked me how I get along with four daughters-in-law. First of all, they are all great women and I love them, but it does take compromising. With respect to how we handle Christmas, I learned a long time ago that it's wise to respect others' family traditions. Many times over the years, the Robertsons would join

Above: Here I am surrounded by my boys. This must be about 1997. I see all the boys are working on that beard thing—just not quite there yet. I'm sure I was cooking, like I always do.

one of the in-law families for a particular holiday, like Easter at Korie's mom's house. I guess in a way, it's easier that I have all sons because I'm not juggling sons-in-law as well! Christmas, for us, means celebrating whenever we can all get together. Some years it's on Christmas Day at the evening meal; some years it's a day or two before Christmas. For me, it's not the particular day that matters; it's that we are all together.

When we do get together for our Christmas celebration, we eat first—but we are never on time. We seem to always wait on someone who's running late or some food to cook properly. We try not to get in a hurry and just enjoy the moment. We chose Cajun food many years ago when the boys wanted something besides the traditional meal. I've always loved shrimp from the time I was little, so the Cajun theme was perfect for me. As all of the kids have grown in their cooking skills, they have also added to the meal.

As I mentioned, our house is small. Phil and I have lived in the same house for close to forty years. Granny and Pa (Phil's parents) helped us buy the property and house we are in now. It originally had two houses. They moved into what was called the "camp house," and we moved into the other house. Somewhere in the early 1990s, we did some remodeling. That's when I got a modern kitchen, complete with a dishwasher. I raised my four boys with one bathroom and no dishwasher. I always thank the Lord that I had boys with that one bathroom!

Above: I'm not sure what year this was, but it's Willie before long hair, so late 1990s. This shows you my "decoration obsession." Could I just put one more thing out? I don't think so! Opposite: I really went "Christmas Crazy" that year. For some reason, I decided a fence was needed in my house to keep the dogs out of the presents. I threw on some tinsel and that was that!

It's very crowded when everyone is at our house, now that we have fourteen grandchildren and two great-grandchildren. So after we devour that good cooking, we all move over to our living room. And literally I mean move over. Our living room and dining area are in the same room. I've seen some modern houses with a floor plan that has the kitchen, dining room, and den all in the same space, but we've had that for years! Anyway, once the tree is added to that, we're packed in like sardines. The men and women take the couches, the teens sit on the armrests of the couches, and the little kids line the floors. Of course Phil has his chair. Then the gift exchange begins. The cousins exchange gifts with one another, and the brothers and wives do as well. I love to give silly or gag gifts to my kids, the boys, and daughters-in-law. We spend the night telling stories and laughing. A domino game is likely to break out as well. And then it's every man for himself, as the Robertson men battle to see who is the "domino king of the year."

Since our TV show began, we've gotten so many comments about our dinner scenes. Of course, we don't do that every night. Each of my children has his own family that he shares a meal with on most nights, but we do get together often, and I wouldn't trade those times for anything. I certainly wouldn't jeopardize the

opportunity by being stubborn about a time or date. Family time is too important for that! Remember to be willing to compromise. It will go a long way toward a healthy and happy relationship with all your family members. 🐦

Quick & Easy Shrimp Salad

Makes 4 servings • Large salad bowl

1 pound boiled shrimp, peeled and
deveined
1½ large celery stalks, finely chopped
3 hard-boiled eggs, peeled and finely
chopped
½ cup mayonnaise
Salt and black pepper

Mix all the ingredients in the bowl. Stir well to
distribute the mayonnaise and seasoning. Chill in
the refrigerator.

A Note from Miss Kay

These days you can get cooked shrimp in most grocery stores, so this recipe is quick and easy to do. If you will notice, most Louisiana dishes are pretty heavy with butter and cream. It's nice to have something light like this shrimp salad.

Fried Shrimp

Deep cast-iron skillet (size will vary according to the number of shrimp you're cooking)

Shrimp, fresh or thawed frozen,
peeled and deveined
Salt, black pepper, and garlic salt
Egg wash (1 large egg for each
½ pound shrimp)
All-purpose flour (½ cup for each
½ pound shrimp)
Peanut oil, for frying

1. Sprinkle the shrimp with a little salt, pepper, and
garlic salt to taste.

2. Roll the shrimp in egg wash, then in flour.

3. Fill the skillet about halfway with oil. Heat to
about 350°F over medium heat.

4. Fry the shrimp (not too many at one time) for
1 minute or until they float to the top. Drain
quickly on paper towels, and add any other
seasoning you like after each batch is fried.

A Note from Miss Kay

This recipe really depends on how many shrimp you have and how many folks you're feeding. Just use more eggs and more flour and a bigger pan, and you're good to go!

Crawfish Pie

Makes 1 (9-inch) pie • Large skillet • 9-inch pie pan

1 stick (¼ pound) butter

1 small onion, finely chopped

1 bell pepper, finely chopped

1 celery stalk, finely chopped

2 tablespoons all-purpose flour

1 can (10.75 ounces) cream of mushroom soup

Pinch each of salt and black pepper

Duck Commander Cajun Seasoning (mild or zesty)

1 pound crawfish tail meat, fresh or thawed frozen

2 (9-inch) piecrusts, homemade (page 182) or store-bought, unbaked

1. Heat the oven to 350°F.

2. In the skillet, melt the butter over medium heat. Add the onion, bell pepper, and celery and cook, stirring occasionally, until very soft, 15 to 20 minutes.

3. Add the flour and stir until the vegetables are coated well. Stir in the soup, salt, pepper, Cajun seasoning, and crawfish tails.

4. Fit one piece of dough into the pie pan, pressing it into the sides to prevent it from slipping down. Bake for 5 minutes, then remove it from the oven.

5. Spoon the crawfish filling into the crust and top with the remaining dough. Pinch the edges together. With a knife, make several slashes in the top for steam vents.

6. Bake until the crust is golden brown and the filling is bubbling, about 30 minutes.

A Note from Miss Kay

The great news about this recipe is that you don't have to wait until peak crawfish season, which is in the spring, to cook it. You can use frozen crawfish tails, and it's just as good. Everyone in our family looks forward to crawfish pie at Christmas. It's a fun and different way to celebrate the season.

Fried Crawfish Patties

Makes 32 patties • Large skillet • Large deep cast-iron skillet

1 stick (¼ pound) butter
2 white onions, diced
¼ cup sliced green onions or scallions
1 bell pepper, diced
2 celery stalks, diced
8 garlic cloves, finely chopped
¼ cup dried parsley flakes
1 teaspoon dried thyme
1 teaspoon dried basil
2 or 3 dashes Louisiana hot sauce
Salt and black pepper
1 pound lump crabmeat, cleaned
1 pound cooked crawfish tail meat,
    thawed if frozen
2 large eggs
About 1½ cups Italian-style bread
    crumbs
⅔ cup all-purpose flour
Peanut oil, for frying

1. In the large skillet, melt the butter over medium heat. Add the white onions, green onions, bell pepper, and celery and cook, stirring occasionally, until the vegetables are soft, 8 to 10 minutes.

2. Stir in the garlic, parsley, thyme, basil, and hot sauce. Transfer to a large bowl and season with salt and pepper. Add the crabmeat, crawfish tails, and eggs and mix well. Stir in enough bread crumbs to hold the mixture together. Make 32 small patties (¼ cup each) and roll them in the flour.

3. Fill the deep skillet about halfway with oil. Heat the oil to 350°F over medium heat. (Drop a pinch of flour in the oil to check the temperature. The flour will sizzle when it's ready.)

4. Working in batches if necessary, carefully add the patties to the oil and cook until golden brown, 3 to 5 minutes. Drain on paper towels.

A Note from Miss Kay
Phil is the best at cooking these delicious treats. He usually cooks them as an appetizer, but we could all eat them for our meal!

Shrimp au Gratin

Makes 12 servings • Large skillet • 12 (6-ounce) custard cups or a regular 12-cup muffin tin

1½ sticks (12 tablespoons) butter, melted

1 onion, chopped

1 bell pepper, chopped

2 celery stalks, chopped

4 garlic cloves, minced

⅓ cup all-purpose flour

1 quart heavy whipping cream, plus more if needed

1 cup shredded cheddar cheese, plus more for the top (optional)

Dash of hot sauce

Salt and black pepper

1½ pounds peeled and deveined cooked shrimp (you can also use crabmeat or crawfish for this recipe)

2 cups Italian-style bread crumbs

1. Heat the oven to 350°F.

2. In the skillet, melt the butter over medium heat. Add the onion, bell pepper, celery, and garlic and cook, stirring occasionally, until the vegetables are tender, about 8 minutes.

3. Add the flour and mix well. Cook on low heat, stirring often, for 2 minutes (do not scorch or brown).

4. Add the cream and cook, stirring frequently, until thickened. If it gets too thick, add more cream; it should look like thick gravy.

5. Add the cheese and stir until it melts. Add the hot sauce and season to taste with salt and pepper. Stir in the shrimp.

6. Pour into the custard cups. Sprinkle the bread crumbs (and a little cheese, if you like) over the top. Bake until bubbly, about 20 minutes.

A Note from Miss Kay

We love shrimp done any way, but au gratin is so delicious! "Au gratin," in English, just means "with cheese," so this is shrimp with cheese. Your family will thank you for making this dish!

Willie's Crazy Bread

Makes 1 loaf • Cookie sheet

1 loaf French bread (12 inches long
   and about 9 ounces)
1 stick (¼ pound) butter, melted
1 cup shredded mozzarella cheese
1 teaspoon garlic salt
4 slices bacon, cut in thirds crosswise

1. Heat the oven to 400°F.

2. Slice the bread about 1 inch thick without cutting
   all the way through. Place the bread on the cookie
   sheet.

3. Pour butter between the slices, then stuff cheese
   between the slices. Sprinkle with garlic salt.
   Top the bread with the bacon slices without
   overlapping them.

4. Bake until the cheese has melted, about 5 minutes.

5. Turn the oven to broil and cook the bacon to your
   taste.

A Note from Willie
*This recipe doesn't help me keep my girlish figure, but it sure is good. I always like to
"experiment" in the kitchen. When I make this, it never makes it to the table. Everyone
is waiting by the oven for it to come out.*

Do-Ahead Piecrusts

Makes enough for 4 (9-inch) pies • Rolling pin
Pastry blender (Just Google "pastry blender" and see what they look like, then buy one at any store.)

**5 cups all-purpose flour, plus more
    for rolling**
1 teaspoon salt
**2¼ cups butter-flavored vegetable
    shortening (Crisco is the best)**
1 large egg
2 tablespoons vinegar
1 cup cold water minus 2 tablespoons

1. In a large mixing bowl, stir together the flour and salt. Mix the shortening into the flour with the pastry blender. Add the egg and mix by hand for a few minutes.

2. Stir the vinegar into the measuring cup with the water. Slowly pour the liquid into the bowl, stirring with a fork. Stir for 2 to 3 minutes to blend everything.

3. Divide the dough into four parts. Wrap any pieces that you aren't using in plastic wrap and refrigerate them.

4. Sprinkle flour on a clean countertop and put down a piece of dough. Sprinkle the dough with flour, and with a rolling pin, roll the dough to about ⅛ inch thick, to fit the pie pan you are using. (For a 9-inch pan, roll the dough to a circle about 12 inches in diameter.) Fit the crust into the pan and gently press it down to fit. Roll as many piecrusts as you need, flouring the counter each time.

5. If your recipe calls for the piecrust to be already baked, bake it at 350°F for 25 minutes.

A Note from Miss Kay

I wasn't sure about including this recipe, because most cooks today are happy with a store-bought piecrust, but I decided you should know how to make one anyway. At Christmastime, you never know when company might be coming and you don't have time to go to the store. And it really isn't that hard. Trust me, you can do it! Note: the apple pie on page 52 has a homemade crust as well.

Alan's Cream Cheese Pie

Makes 1 (9-inch) pie • Electric mixer

1 package (8 ounces) cream cheese, softened

1 can (14 ounces) sweetened condensed milk (I use Eagle)

⅓ cup lemon juice

1 store-bought 9-inch graham cracker crust or make your own (recipe for Easy Vanilla Wafer Piecrust below)

1 can (21 ounces) cherry pie filling, or your favorite fruit pie filling

1. In a large mixing bowl, with the electric mixer, beat the cream cheese until fluffy. Add the condensed milk and lemon juice, and beat until no lumps remain. Pour into the prepared piecrust and refrigerate for at least four hours. Overnight is best.

2. Top with the pie filling.

A Note from Miss Kay

Even the grandkids request Alan's pie year-round, not just at Christmas! Yep, this man's a keeper! Good looking, loves his wife and family, loves God, and cooks!

Easy Vanilla Wafer Piecrust

Makes enough for 1 (9-inch) pie • 9-inch pie pan

1 cup crushed vanilla wafers

¾ stick (6 tablespoons) butter, melted

½ cup pecans, crushed

1. Heat the oven to 350°F.

2. In a medium mixing bowl, mix all ingredients together. Pat into the bottom and up the sides of a 9-inch pie pan. Bake 12 to 15 minutes until golden brown, then line the sides with vanilla wafers. Let cool before filling.

A Note from Miss Kay

Here's another great piecrust that's easy to whip up. You can also use it for Alan's pie on page 38 or for any cream-type pie.

Carrot Cake

Makes 1 (9-inch) cake • Electric mixer • 3 (9-inch) round cake pans • Wire cooling racks
Nonstick cooking spray and flour, for the pans

Cake

2 cups all-purpose flour
2 teaspoons ground cinnamon
2 teaspoons baking soda
2 teaspoons baking powder
1 teaspoon salt
2 cups sugar
1½ cups vegetable oil
4 large eggs
3 cups grated carrots (about 1 pound)
½ cups chopped pecans

Cream Cheese Frosting

1 stick (¼ pound) butter, softened
1 (8 ounce) package cream cheese, softened
2 teaspoons vanilla extract
1 package (1 pound) powdered sugar, sifted

1. Heat the oven to 325°F. Grease and flour the cake pans.

2. Make the cake: In a large mixing bowl, sift together the flour, cinnamon, baking soda, baking powder, and salt.

3. In another large bowl, with the electric mixer, beat the sugar and oil until well combined. Add the eggs one at a time, beating well after each addition.

4. Sift the dry ingredients into the sugar mixture. Stir in the carrots and pecans; mix well.

5. Pour the batter into the pans. Bake until the layers start to pull away at the sides and a toothpick inserted in the center of a layer comes out clean, about 45 minutes.

6. Let the layers cool in the pans for a few minutes, then run a spatula around the sides and invert onto wire racks to cool completely.

7. While the layers are cooling, make the frosting: Beat together the butter, cream cheese, vanilla, and sugar with the mixer until fluffy. (The frosting will appear stiff at first, but will soften as you mix it.)

8. When the cake layers are cool, frost the top of one layer, then place another layer over it, frosting that layer, then put the last layer on top. Frost the top and sides.

A Note from Miss Kay

I love a good recipe for carrot cake with cream cheese icing, and this one is excellent! Even "anti-carrot" people will love this cake. Our family does!

Phil's Famous Eggnog

Makes 8 servings • Electric mixer • Mugs, chilled in the freezer, for serving

6 large eggs, separated
1 tablespoon sugar
1 to 1½ quarts vanilla ice cream,
softened
½ cup bourbon (don't worry, it's just
a tad)
Freshly grated nutmeg

1. In a large bowl, with the electric mixer, beat the egg whites until stiff peaks form. (The peaks will stay standing when you remove the beaters.)

2. In a separate bowl, with the mixer (you don't have to wash the beaters), beat the egg yolks and sugar on high speed for 7 to 8 minutes, until the mixture is very thick and falls in ribbons when you lift the beaters.

3. Using a large spoon, add the ice cream to the egg yolks. With the mixer, beat on low until it is the consistency of a malt, thick and creamy. Dribble in the bourbon (just a bit to taste), mixing on low speed.

4. Gently fold in the beaten egg whites by hand.

5. Serve immediately in frozen mugs with nutmeg sprinkled on top.

A Note from Phil

This eggnog is best eaten with a spoon. We have it only twice a year—Christmas and New Year's Eve. It's definitely on everyone's wish list.

Jessica's Banana Liqueur Cake

Makes 1 Bundt cake • Bundt pan (10 to 12 cups) • Electric mixer • Medium saucepan
Nonstick cooking spray and flour, for the pan

Cake

1 box (16.5 ounces) yellow cake mix
½ cup vegetable oil
½ cup water
½ cup crème de banana liqueur
4 large eggs
1 box (3.4 ounces) French vanilla pudding mix
1 cup coarsely chopped pecans

Topping

½ cup crème de banana liqueur
¼ cup water
1 cup sugar
1 stick (¼ pound) butter
¼ cup finely chopped pecans

1. Heat the oven to 325°F. Grease and flour the Bundt pan.

2. Make the cake: In a large bowl, with the electric mixer, beat the cake mix, oil, water, liqueur, eggs, and pudding together until well combined.

3. Pour the nuts into the bottom of the Bundt pan. Pour the cake batter over the nuts.

4. Bake until the cake starts to pull away at the sides and a toothpick inserted near the center comes out clean, about 1 hour. Remove from the oven, but leave the cake in the pan.

5. When the cake is almost done baking, make the topping: In a medium saucepan, bring the liqueur, water, sugar, and butter to a boil over high heat. Boil three minutes.

6. Stir in the pecans and quickly pour the mixture over the hot cake in the pan.

7. Let stand for 25 minutes, then invert onto a cake plate.

A Note from Miss Kay

Time to brag on my daughters-in-law. This is Jessica's contribution to our Christmas dinner, and it is de-li-cious! If you want to impress your in-laws with your cooking, make this cake!

10.

Wild Game Cooking

〜〜〜〜〜〜〜〜〜〜〜〜〜〜〜〜〜〜

He is richest who is content

with the least, for content is

the wealth of nature.

—Socrates

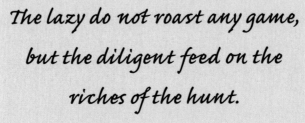

The lazy do not roast any game,
but the diligent feed on the
riches of the hunt.

—Proverbs 12:27, NIV

Wild Game Recipes

Wild Hog for Supper

As the story goes, Phil killed his first—actually two—ducks at eleven years of age. At the time, he had no retriever or boat to bring in his bounty, so he took off his clothes and waded through the ice-cold water. This is just one of the stories told about my "backwoods" boyfriend when we started dating.

By the time we married, I was aware of Phil's hunting philosophy: if it flew, grew wild, swam, or lived in a tree, it belonged to whoever could catch it. So I shouldn't have been surprised when a wild hog appeared for supper. We had bought a huge black pot at a garage sale, and Phil was determined to boil that wild hog into a tasty treat. But it was a boar hog and the longer Phil boiled it, the worse the smell got in our little apartment. I'm convinced that even our own Duck Commander spices wouldn't have covered up the smell of that boar hog!

Hours went by, with Phil adding more water to the boiling pot of stinky pig. Then I started to get sick. That was it, as far as I was concerned. Even if Phil had managed to get the meat a little easier to chew, I wasn't going to eat it. After some newly-married-type pleading, I persuaded Phil not only to throw out that boar but to throw out the pot as well!

Above: Phil had just started teaching and coaching at Ouachita Christian School when he caught this bobcat. No, we did not eat it!

Well, not all things in life can be, or are worth being saved. There have been many things in our life together that we have had to let go. Some of them have been easy for me and not for Phil, some of them the other way around. Some have involved friendships, family members, our business, and long-held church beliefs. But through prayers and God's guidance, we have helped each other work through every situation, and when it's time to "throw out the pot," we do it together.

In every marriage, there will be things worth holding on to for all they're worth, and there will be things that need, as Phil says it, to be culled. After over forty years, we have worked through so many of those things. If you are newly married, don't be so quick to cull what is worth saving. Be wise. Ask God for guidance. Seek wise counsel. And always know there is hope!

Above: The boys decided to build the world's largest duck call for our fortieth-anniversary party. I think Phil was proud of it.

Wild Turkey Tenders

Makes 8 to 10 servings • Deep-fryer

8 to 10 turkey tenders (the number can vary according to your family needs)

Salt and black pepper

3 cups all-purpose flour

3 large eggs

1 cup buttermilk

Peanut or canola oil, for frying

Duck Commander Cajun Seasoning (mild or zesty) or other Cajun seasoning (optional)

1. Cut the turkey tenders crosswise into ⅓-inch-wide strips. Salt and pepper the turkey strips and roll them in flour.

2. In a shallow bowl, whisk together the eggs and buttermilk.

3. Dip the turkey strips in the egg mixture to coat, then immediately roll them again in fresh flour. (This will make the crust stick to the meat, locking in moisture.)

4. Fill the deep-fryer with oil according to the manufacturer's directions and heat it to 375°F.

5. Fry strips until golden brown, about 3 minutes.

6. Remove from the oil and drain on paper towels. Season with salt and pepper. If you like a spicier taste, sprinkle with Cajun seasoning immediately after cooking.

A Note from Miss Kay

With recipes like this one, there's no need to wait for Thanksgiving to eat turkey. It's easy to make and delicious!

Swamp-Seasoned Fried Duck

Meat mallet • Large deep cast-iron skillet

Skinless duck breast fillets (any number you have shot or been given)

All-purpose flour

Salt and black pepper

Duck Commander Cajun Seasoning (mild or zesty) or other Cajun seasoning

Milk

Vegetable oil, for frying

1. Soak wild duck breasts in fresh water for 3 days in the refrigerator, changing the water several times. (If using domestic duck, there's no need to soak.) After 3 days, the meat should look gray instead of dark red.

2. With a meat mallet, pound the breasts to ½ inch thick.

3. Season flour with salt, pepper, and Cajun seasoning. Dip the breasts in milk, then roll in the seasoned flour.

4. Fill the skillet about halfway with oil. Heat to about 350°F over medium heat. Add the duck and cook until golden brown on both sides, about 6 to 8 minutes per side. Drain on paper towels.

A Note from Phil
Say grace, serve, and enjoy!

Boiled Squirrel & Dumplings

This is the best way to cook older squirrel—the big ones.

Makes 8 servings • Large (10- to 14-quart) soup pot with a lid • Pastry blender (optional) • Rolling pin

Broth & Squirrel

1 large squirrel, skinned and cut in
half (if you can't get squirrel, use a
large rabbit or large chicken)
Salt and black pepper
1 can (12 ounces) evaporated milk
½ stick (4 tablespoons) butter

Dumplings

4 cups all-purpose flour, plus more
for rolling
5 teaspoons baking powder
1 teaspoon salt
¾ teaspoon baking soda
3 tablespoons butter-flavored
vegetable shortening (I use Crisco)
2 cups buttermilk

A Note from Miss Kay
*You might not like squirrel
or have access to squirrel,
but you can use this
dumpling recipe with chicken just
as well. Boil your chicken or buy a
precooked rotisserie chicken. Either
way, it's a dish your family will love.*

1. Make the broth and squirrel: In the soup pot,
bring 10 cups of water to a boil. Add the squirrel
and season generously with salt and pepper.
Cover and simmer until tender enough to be
pierced with a fork, about 1 hour.

2. Remove the squirrel from the broth and set aside.
Add the milk and butter to the broth. Leave the
broth to simmer while you make the dumplings.

3. Make the dumplings: In a large mixing bowl,
sift together the flour, baking powder, salt, and
baking soda. With a pastry blender or 2 knives
scissor-fashion, cut in the shortening until
the mixture resembles coarse crumbs. Add the
buttermilk a little at a time, stirring until a soft
dough forms, about like the consistency of biscuit
dough. Divide the dough into 4 balls.

4. Sprinkle the counter with flour. Roll each ball of
dough to ⅛- to ¼-inch thick, adding more flour as
needed to prevent it from sticking. Cut into large
squares.

5. Return the broth to a boil. Make sure there is
enough in the pot to fill at least half the pot. If
not, add more water.

6. Drop the dumplings into the boiling broth a handful
at a time. When they are all in, turn the heat to
low, cover the pot, and simmer for 15 minutes.

7. Turn off the heat. Put the meat back in the pot
and let it sit until hot again.

Phil's Duck Gumbo

Makes 10 to 15 servings • Large (10- to 14-quart) soup pot with a lid • Large (7- to 8-quart) cooking pot

4 wood ducks or 6 teal or 3 mallards; plucked, eviscerated, and cleaned, heads and feet removed

Salt and black pepper

3 bay leaves

2 cups peanut oil

2 cups all-purpose flour

3 white onions, chopped

3 green onions or scallions, chopped

3 celery stalks, chopped

6 garlic cloves, chopped

A handful of fresh parsley, chopped

Duck Commander Cajun Seasoning (mild or zesty) or other Cajun seasoning

1 package (24 ounces) hot pork sausage, diced nickel-size (we use Savoie's)

1 package (24 ounces) andouille sausage, diced nickel-size

1 package (28 ounces) frozen whole okra

1. Place the ducks in the soup pot filled with water. Add the salt and pepper to taste, and the bay leaves. Bring to a boil, lower to a simmer, and cook until the ducks are tender but not falling apart, about 2 hours.

2. Remove the ducks from the broth and set aside. Reserve the broth (discard the bay leaves). When the ducks are cool enough to handle, skin them and remove the meat from the bones; discard the skin and bones.

3. While your ducks are cooking, in the large cooking pot, heat the oil over medium-low heat. Add the flour and cook, stirring frequently, until the roux is a dark chocolate color, 35 to 40 minutes.

4. Add the white and green onions, celery, garlic, and parsley to the roux. Add enough of the reserved broth to fill it just over half full, and bring it to a boil. Skim off any oil that rises to the surface.

5. Add the Cajun seasoning along with the hot pork sausage, andouille, and duck meat. Simmer 2 hours, then add the okra and simmer 1 hour longer or until all the meat is tender and the gumbo has thickened.

A Note from Phil

I would say the Duck Commander not having a duck gumbo recipe would be as strange as a cell phone in a duck blind. Duck gumbo takes a little work, but it's worth it. Just follow it step by step, and you'll do just fine.

Fried Deer Steak

Meat mallet • Large deep cast-iron skillet

Deer steaks

½ cup buttermilk for every 1 pound deer steaks

1 large egg for every 1 pound deer steaks

1 cup all-purpose flour for every 1 pound deer steaks

Salt and black pepper

Peanut oil or canola oil, for frying

Sliced green onions or scallions, for serving

1. Prepare the deer steaks by beating them one lick on each side with a meat mallet.

2. In a large bowl, whisk together the buttermilk and eggs. In another bowl, season the flour with salt and pepper. Dip the steaks in the milk mixture, then in the seasoned flour.

3. Fill the skillet halfway with oil and heat to 350°F over medium-high heat. Add the steaks and cook until golden brown, about 3 minutes.

4. Drain the steaks on paper towels. Sprinkle with green onions to serve.

A Note from Phil

If the deer is a young deer, you can eat it as soon as you fry it. But if the deer is old, fry it and then layer it in a Dutch oven with a layer of onions and a layer of mushrooms. Cover the pan and bake in the oven at 350°F for an hour.

Fabulous Frog Legs

Makes 2 to 3 servings • Large cast-iron skillet • Dutch oven

6 large or 8 medium frog legs

3 cups buttermilk

2 large eggs

¾ cup beer (½ bottle or can)

3 or 4 dashes of hot sauce

1 tablespoon Worcestershire sauce

2 tablespoons spicy mustard

Salt and black pepper

2 cups all-purpose flour

½ stick (4 tablespoons) butter

6 tablespoons olive oil

3 green onions or scallions, thinly sliced

1 tablespoon chopped parsley

8 to 12 whole garlic cloves, peeled

Duck Commander Cajun Seasoning (mild or zesty) or other Cajun seasoning

1. Heat the oven to 300°F.

2. In a large bowl, cover frog legs with buttermilk. Marinate 1 hour, then drain. Return the frog legs to the bowl.

3. Mix together the eggs, beer, hot sauce, Worcestershire sauce, spicy mustard, and salt and pepper to taste, and pour the mixture over the frog legs. Make sure they are coated completely.

4. One at a time, take out the legs and roll each leg in the flour.

5. In a large cast-iron skillet, melt the butter in 4 tablespoons of the oil over medium heat. Cook the frog legs, turning once, until golden brown on both sides (2 to 3 minutes per side). Remove from the skillet and drain lightly.

6. Pour the remaining 2 tablespoons of oil into the bottom of the Dutch oven, then add the frog legs. Cover them with the green onions, parsley, and garlic and sprinkle with Cajun seasoning to taste.

7. Cover with a lid and bake for 15 to 20 minutes, until the frog legs are tender.

A Note from Miss Kay

Eating frog legs might sound pretty redneck to most of you readers, but truly, they are delicious. Don't think about the little frog hopping by your back door. The frogs my boys catch have legs as big as chicken legs. And do they taste like chicken? Well, to me, they taste like frog legs.

Squirrel with Soup Gravy

Makes 8 servings • Dutch oven

Peanut oil, for frying

4 squirrels, cleaned and cut into pieces

Salt and black pepper

1 cup all-purpose flour

1 can (14.5 ounces) chicken broth

2 cans (10.75 ounces each) French onion soup

2 cans (10.75 ounces each) cream of mushroom soup

1 cup water

Just Right White Rice (page 110), for serving

1. Heat the oven to 300°F.

2. Fill a Dutch oven a quarter of the way up with oil; heat to medium. Season the squirrels with salt and pepper and coat with ½ cup of the flour. Fry the squirrel pieces until golden brown on all sides. Remove and set aside.

3. Pour out most of the oil from frying the squirrels, leaving ½ inch in the pot. Add the remaining ½ cup flour and cook over medium heat, stirring frequently, until the roux turns a rich golden brown, about 12 minutes.

4. Pour in the chicken broth and simmer until it reaches a gravy consistency. Stir in the onion soup, mushroom soup, and water. Return the squirrels to the pot, bring to a simmer, cover, and place in the oven. Bake until the squirrels are tender, about 2 hours.

5. Serve over rice.

A Note from Miss Kay

If you have never thought you'd like squirrel, you might surprise yourself after eating this delicious meal. It's one of Phil's best. In Louisiana it's not unusual for people to eat squirrel. Korie grew up in one of those "yuppie" neighborhoods, as Phil would say, and her papaw cooked squirrel for breakfast. I guess she was in training for our family. Plus, the soup gravy is delicious!

Duck & Dressing

Makes about 15 servings • Large (7- to 8-quart) cooking pot with a lid • Large cast-iron skillet • Roasting pan

Duck

8 teal or 3 mallards or 1 large chicken

3 bay leaves

4 garlic cloves

Salt and black pepper

Dressing

1 stick (¼ pound) butter

2 medium onions, diced

2 bell peppers, diced

3 celery stalks, diced

2 pans Cornbread (page 224, or use any recipe you like to get 16 cups), crumbled

1 sleeve saltine crackers, crushed

1 sleeve Ritz crackers, crushed

10 slices white bread, toasted in the oven and crumbled

1 can (12 ounces) evaporated milk (we use Pet)

4 large eggs, beaten

1 heaping teaspoon rubbing sage

1. Make the duck: In the large pot, combine the ducks, bay leaves, garlic, and salt and pepper to taste. Add water to cover by 2 inches and bring to a boil over high heat. Lower to a simmer, cover, and cook for 1 hour and 45 minutes or until the ducks are tender. Set aside the ducks, covered with foil. Save the broth.

2. Heat the oven to 325°F.

3. Make the dressing: In the large skillet, melt the butter over medium heat. Add the onions, bell peppers, and celery and cook, stirring occasionally, until the vegetables are tender, about 7 minutes.

4. In the roasting pan, using your hands, combine the cornbread, saltines, Ritz crackers, and white bread. Add the vegetables and mix well. Add duck broth slowly until the dressing is pourable but still thick. Add the evaporated milk, eggs, and sage; mix well with a large kitchen spoon.

5. Place the ducks on the dressing, breast side up. Push the ducks down into the dressing, but leave the breast showing. Bake uncovered for 45 minutes.

A Note from Miss Kay

We wouldn't be the Duck Commander family without lots of duck recipes. If you have duck hunters in your family, you will love this recipe. Of course, it's similar to turkey and dressing, but we get to use all those ducks my guys bring in.

Willie's Armadillo Eggs

Makes 6 to 16 servings • Outdoor grill (optional)

6 to 8 large jalapeño peppers, cut in half lengthwise, seeds and ribs removed

1 package (8 ounces) cream cheese, softened

2 pounds breakfast sausage, formed into 12 to 16 patties

1 pound bacon, sliced thin

1 stick (¼ pound) butter, melted

1. If you're using a grill, heat it to medium. If not, heat the oven to 400°F.

2. Fill each jalapeño half with cream cheese. Mold sausage around each jalapeño half, making sure to cover the entire jalapeño. Wrap each "armadillo egg" with a slice of bacon.

3. Cook the eggs on an open grill until the sausage is cooked through and the bacon is crispy. If you don't have an outdoor grill, bake in the oven for 15 to 20 minutes, then broil until the bacon is crispy.

4. Remove the eggs from the grill or oven and cover with melted butter.

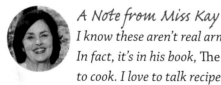

A Note from Miss Kay

I know these aren't real armadillo eggs; I just love the name! Willie uses this recipe a lot. In fact, it's in his book, The Duck Commander Family, *along with other things he likes to cook. I love to talk recipes with Willie. I am so proud that he loves to cook and eat—just like I do!*

11.

Remembering Granny

If God had intended us to

follow recipes, He wouldn't have

given us grandmothers.

—Linda Henley

No widow may be put on the list of widows unless she is over sixty, has been faithful to her husband, and is well known for her good deeds, such as bringing up children, showing hospitality, washing the feet of the Lord's people, helping those in trouble and devoting herself to all kinds of good deeds.

—1 Timothy 5:9–10, NIV

Remembering Granny

〰〰〰〰〰〰〰〰〰〰〰〰〰〰〰〰〰〰

Granny & Iced Tea

Phil's mom wasn't always called Granny. Her name was Merritt, like one of my granddaughters (*pictured at left*). She was a tough lady who raised five boys and two girls through some very hard years. It's difficult for me to hear young people complain today when I think of Granny and how she clothed and fed those seven children on next to nothing.

In the early years, Granny and Pa lived in a four-room log cabin where four of the boys slept in the same bed. There was no air-conditioning or heat and the running water came through a single hose that Pa had rigged up through a window in the kitchen. Since there was no hot water, Granny had to put on a big pot of water to boil every morning. That was used for everything from cleaning the dishes to bathing the children.

Most of the food they ate was raised on their own plot of land. Hogs provided bacon, cows provided milk, butter, and beef, chickens (bought by mail order for $5.00 per 100) provided eggs, and a garden provided a variety of vegetables. Beyond that, the boys hunted and fished and, for all they knew, they had more than enough. Granny and Pa were hardworking

Above: Granny and Pa with all their grandchildren. See if you can spot my boys. Here's a clue: Alan has a mustache, Willie is preppy, Jase is serious, and Jep is little.

folks who raised their children to work hard, too, and to value what they had been blessed with.

The first time I ate at Granny's house, I was eager to show her that I could help out in the kitchen. I asked repeatedly for her to give me a job. I'm sure she was hesitant to turn the food preparation over to a fifteen-year-old, so she told me my job was to put the ice in the glasses. She made that job sound so special by telling me that no tea tastes good until it is poured into a clean glass filled to the top with fresh ice. I proudly did my job to the best of my ability.

Over the years, Granny taught me many lessons in cooking, but more important, she taught me life lessons. One lesson I'll never forget is how she cleaned up her brood of children every Sunday and, with nine people in one car, headed to church. Granny made sure her children didn't go physically hungry, but she did want them to be hungry for the Word of God. I'm pretty sure she succeeded. All seven of her children are faithful believers.

Granny was quite the character. In her older years, she loved the game show *The Price Is Right*, and was chosen to be on the show in 1999. She even won a car! Thank you, Granny, for leaving a legacy of working hard, holding on to family, and honoring God in all you do.

*Top: This is the Robertson Seven! From youngest to oldest: Jan, Si, Phil, Tommy, Judy, Harold, and Jimmy Frank. Now, that's a good-looking bunch! **Above right**: Granny is pictured with her oldest daughter, Judy. Granny lived with Judy the last few years of her life.*

Sour Cream Cake

Makes 1 Bundt cake • Bundt pan (10 to 12 cups) • Wire cooling rack • Nonstick cooking spray and flour, for the pan

1 box (16.5 ounces) Duncan Hines
    Butter Cake mix

⅔ cup vegetable oil

½ cup sugar

1 carton (8 ounces) sour cream

4 large eggs

2 teaspoons vanilla extract

1. Heat the oven to 350°F. Grease and flour the Bundt pan.

2. In a large mixing bowl, combine the cake mix, oil, sugar, and sour cream. Add the eggs one at a time, beating well after each addition. Stir in the vanilla.

3. Pour the batter into the pan. Bake until the cake starts to pull away at the sides and a toothpick inserted near the center comes out clean, about 45 minutes.

4. Let the cake cool in the pan for a few minutes, then invert onto a wire rack to cool completely. If you're in a hurry, put it right on a cake plate.

A Note from Miss Kay

This cake is delicious just as it is or with a glaze of some kind. One of my favorites is a simple one. Just use 1 cup powdered sugar, ¼ teaspoon grated orange zest, and 1 to 2 tablespoons orange juice. Mix that up and pour it over the top of the cake while it's still warm.

Chili with Beans

Makes 4 to 6 servings • Dutch oven

2 pounds hamburger meat
2 teaspoons salt
3 tablespoons chili powder
2 tablespoons all-purpose flour
1 teaspoon red pepper flakes (optional)
2 cans (15 ounces each) tomato sauce
1 cup water
1 can (15 ounces) pinto beans, drained

1. In the Dutch oven, brown the meat over medium heat. Drain off any grease that remains.

2. Add the salt, chili powder, flour, red pepper flakes (if using), tomato sauce, water, and beans and bring to a boil. Lower to a simmer, cover, and cook 1 hour, until thickened.

A Note from Miss Kay

This is a simple chili recipe, but it will warm you up on a cold day. Of course, double it if you need to, and serve with crackers.

Pineapple Cheese Salad

Makes 10 servings • Serving platter

Fancy leaf lettuce, washed and dried
1 can (20 ounces) sliced pineapple, drained
Grated cheddar cheese
Mayonnaise
Maraschino cherries

Tear the lettuce into 10 pieces, each about the size of your palm, and lay on the platter to make individual servings. Cover each lettuce piece with a slice of pineapple. Sprinkle cheese on top of each pineapple ring. Place a dab of mayonnaise on top of the cheese and top with a cherry.

A Note from Miss Kay

I can't explain it, but this was and is one of my favorite dishes handed down by Granny. I'm sure at the time it was a fairly inexpensive way to make a fancier salad and to get your kids to eat lettuce and fruit. I've always been partial to maraschino cherries, so that's probably why I love it. Chrys, Korie's mom, said her mother used to do the same thing with pears. That sounds good, too. As long as it's topped with a cherry, I know I'll love it!

Buttermilk Biscuits

Makes about 22 to 24 (3-inch) biscuits • Rolling pin
Baking sheet with ½-inch sides, or 2 (9-inch) round cake pans

4 cups all-purpose flour, plus more for rolling

5 teaspoons baking powder

1 teaspoon salt

¾ teaspoon baking soda

3 tablespoons vegetable shortening (I use Crisco), melted and cooled

2 cups buttermilk

2 tablespoons vegetable oil

1. Heat the oven to 425°F.

2. In a medium bowl, sift together the flour, baking powder, salt, and baking soda. Add the shortening and slowly stir in enough buttermilk (usually just less than 2 cups) to make the dough into a ball.

3. Sprinkle the counter with flour and turn the dough out of the bowl. Roll the dough in the flour until you can manage it without it sticking to your hands. Add more flour on the surface if needed. With a rolling pin covered in flour, roll the dough to ¼ inch thick.

4. Stop here and put your pan in the oven with the vegetable oil. (This oil will be used to dip the biscuits in, making the tops crispy.)

5. Use a biscuit cutter or small round glass dipped in flour to cut the biscuits.

6. Remove the pan from the oven. Dip the top of each biscuit in the oil, then put the biscuit bottom side down on the pan. Repeat with all biscuits.

7. Bake for 12 to 15 minutes, just until they are golden brown.

A Note from Miss Kay

As you can tell, we love our biscuits in this family. I'm sure that's due to the delicious jams and jellies we like to make. Traditionally, southern women learn how to cook biscuits from their mothers and grandmothers, as biscuits used to be made every morning. What wasn't eaten at breakfast would end up on someone's dinner plate.

Rice Pudding

Makes 8 servings • 9x13-inch casserole dish • Butter or nonstick cooking spray, for greasing the casserole

Butter or nonstick cooking spray, for greasing the casserole

2 to 3 cups cooked rice (leftover works great)

1½ cups sugar

3 large eggs

1 cup milk

½ teaspoon ground cinnamon or grated nutmeg

¾ teaspoon vanilla extract

Raisins, optional

1. Heat the oven to 350°F. Grease the casserole.

2. In a large mixing bowl, stir together the rice, sugar, and eggs, stirring until well combined. Stir in the milk, cinnamon, vanilla, and raisins if using. Pour into the casserole.

3. Bake until the center of the pudding is set and the top is golden brown, about 45 minutes.

A Note from Miss Kay

Alan was the first of my children married and he and his wife, Lisa, were the ones most affected by Granny's cooking. Granny lived on one side of us, and just after they got married, Alan and Lisa lived on the other side. It made for some interesting times with one couple just starting out and one wrapping up their lives. Granny was always trying to teach the young wives how to cook, whether they wanted it or not. Now I know they appreciated it and wish she was still around.

Mayhaw Jelly

1 quart juice makes 3 (1-pint) jars of jelly • Heavy-bottomed large saucepan • Cheesecloth
1-pint canning jars with lids

Mayhaw berries

Spring water

1 package Sure-Jell powdered pectin
for every quart of juice

5 cups sugar for every quart of juice

1. Prepare the berries: Pick through and wash the berries several times to remove dirt. Put the berries in the large pot.

2. Almost fill the pot with spring water, leaving 1 inch of the berries uncovered. Put on the stove and turn on the heat to medium-high. Bring to a boil. When the water boils, turn the temperature to low and simmer the berries for about 10 minutes.

3. Use a mallet or anything you have to crush the berries to get the juice out. Let the juice mix with the water.

4. Place a piece of cheesecloth inside a colander and place the colander over a large container. Pour the crushed berries and juice into the colander a little at a time, straining juice through the cheesecloth. Let the juice drain until no more drips through. Gather the cheesecloth into a ball and press gently to get the last of the juice out. (For each batch you'll need 1 quart juice; if you are a little short, add water.) Throw away the crushed berries.

5. Sterilize 3 jars in the oven at 220°F for 20 minutes. Wash the lids well and leave them in hot water.

6. Make the jelly: Pour 1 quart berry juice into a large pot. (Make sure to use a large pot, or it may boil over.) Add the pectin and bring to a boil. When it gets to a rolling boil, pour in the sugar, stirring constantly. Bring to a full rolling boil that can't be stirred down, and boil for exactly 1 minute—no more. Remove from the heat and immediately skim any foam from the top.

7. Pour into the hot jars, leaving ¼ inch headroom at the top, and seal with lids. (The jars must be hot so the boiling berry juice will not crack them.) Process in a boiling-water bath.

8. Repeat until all the berry juice is used.

> *Tip* If you can't get mayhaw berries, use cranberries—that'll get you pretty close.

A Note from Phil

I can remember making jelly as a child. Everyone in our family pitched in to make jelly, as well as to can vegetables. It's how we ate. Momma always had a hot skillet of homemade biscuits for us to eat with our jelly. Nothing like it!

Hale Fries

Makes 8 servings • Dutch oven or large skillet with a lid

Bacon drippings or peanut oil

4 large russet (baking) potatoes
(about 10 ounces each), peeled
and sliced ⅛-inch thick like a
potato chip

Seasonings of your choice: salt, black
pepper, and/or Duck Commander
Cajun Seasoning (mild or zesty)

Fill a Dutch oven with either bacon drippings
(best) or peanut oil to come ¼ inch up the sides.
Add the potatoes and coat with seasonings. Cover
and cook over medium-low heat, turning the
potatoes every 3 to 4 minutes and adding more
seasonings as you go, for about 12 minutes total.

A Note from Phil

*This is an old family recipe from the Hale's, who were on my mother's side of the family.
Everyone in our family could make Hale fries. They go with any kind of meat. And if
company's coming, just peel a few more potatoes!*

Cornbread

Makes 8 servings • Large cast-iron skillet

Bacon drippings or vegetable oil
2½ cups regular yellow cornmeal (not self-rising)
½ cup all-purpose flour
2 tablespoons sugar
1½ teaspoons salt
1 teaspoon baking soda
1 large egg
2¼ cups buttermilk

1. Heat the oven to 425°F. While you are mixing the cornbread batter, pour enough bacon drippings or oil into the skillet to cover the bottom and heat it up on the stove. Heat the skillet until a drop of cornbread batter sizzles.

2. In a large mixing bowl, combine the cornmeal, flour, sugar, salt, and baking soda. In a separate bowl, whisk together the egg and buttermilk. Stir that into the cornmeal mixture. Pour the batter into the sizzling hot skillet and bake until golden brown, about 20 minutes.

A Note from Miss Kay

Cornbread is another southern delicacy that most of the cooks in Louisiana add to a plate of summer vegetables. Cornbread goes way back in American history to the American Indians who harvested corn. We are thankful for that little discovery and to the Indians for sharing it. A cast-iron skillet is really the key here, so it might be time for you to invest in one. It will be worth it!

Hot Water Cornbread

Makes about 8 pieces • Large cast-iron skillet

2½ cups regular yellow cornmeal (not self-rising)
1 teaspoon salt
½ cup all-purpose flour
1 teaspoon sugar
3 cups boiling water
Peanut or vegetable oil, for frying

1. In a medium mixing bowl, stir together the cornmeal, salt, flour, and sugar. Stirring constantly, pour in boiling water just until the cornmeal mixture is wet but not runny. (You might not use all the water.)

2. Pour oil into the skillet to come ¼ of the way up the sides. Place over medium heat. (Don't start this too soon, so the oil won't burn.)

3. Put your hands in cold water, because the batter will be hot, and scoop out a small handful of batter. Form it into a flat patty, then drop it in the hot oil. Keep making patties until the skillet is full. Fry until golden brown, turning once, about 2 minutes per side.

4. Drain on paper towels. Repeat until you've used all the batter.

A Note from Miss Kay

Hot water cornbread can be tricky to make, but once mastered, it is so good. The trick is to have your grease really hot so your mixture doesn't turn to mush. Serve with ham or pork chops, and your family will sing your praises!

Blackberry Jam Cake

Makes 1 (9x13-inch) cake • 9x13-inch cake pan • Electric mixer • Medium saucepan
Nonstick cooking spray and flour, for the pan

Cake

2 cups sugar
2 sticks (½ pound) butter, softened
   (do not use margarine)
4 large eggs, separated
1 teaspoon vanilla extract
3 cups all-purpose flour
1 teaspoon baking soda
2 teaspoons ground cinnamon
1 teaspoon grated nutmeg
1 teaspoon ground cloves
1 teaspoon ground allspice
1 cup buttermilk
1 cup blackberry jam

Caramel Frosting

1 cup whole milk
1 cup evaporated milk (I use Pet)
2 cups sugar
2 tablespoons butter
1 teaspoon vanilla extract
1 cup candied cherries
1 cup coarsely chopped nuts
   (we like pecans or walnuts)

A Note from Miss Kay
This recipe was a favorite
of Granny's, and it makes
a beautiful cake!

1. Heat the oven to 425°F. Grease and flour the cake pan.

2. Make the cake: In a large bowl, with the electric mixer, beat the sugar and butter until creamy.

3. Add egg yolks and vanilla and beat until blended.

4. Sift together the flour, baking soda, cinnamon, nutmeg, cloves, and allspice. Add the flour mixture and buttermilk alternately to the creamed butter, beginning and ending with the flour.

5. Add the blackberry jam and mix well.

6. In a separate bowl, beat the egg whites to stiff peaks with the mixer. (The peaks will stay standing when you remove the beaters.) Gently fold into the batter.

7. Pour the batter into the pan. Bake until the cake starts to pull away at the sides and a toothpick inserted in the center comes out clean, about 40 minutes.

8. Let the cake cool in the pan for a few minutes, then run a spatula around the sides and invert onto a wire rack to cool completely.

9. Make the frosting: Cook the whole and evaporated milks, sugar, and butter in the saucepan over medium heat, stirring constantly, until a soft ball forms. Stir in the vanilla, cherries, and nuts. Frost the cake immediately, before the caramel hardens.

Thank-Yous

I want to thank Philis Boultinghouse, senior editor with Howard Books, for being a lifelong friend and now a champion of my cookbook.

Thank you to the entire team at Simon & Schuster, which has been instrumental in making my dream come true, and a special thanks to Amanda Demastus, who worked tirelessly on managing many of the details that helped bring this book together.

Thank you to the amazing food photographer, Jennifer Davick, who brought my recipes to life, and to Russell Graves, who traveled to West Monroe to capture a little of our life in his photography.

Many, many thanks to my dearest friends at White's Ferry Road Church, who volunteered to cook and taste my recipes and give us clear instructions on what each one needed.

Thank you to my sweet muffin group for giving me a place to share my life story and for being willing to be a part of this book.

Thank you to my Nanny and Phil's granny for being grandmothers who weren't afraid to speak the truth and who taught me as much about life as they did about cooking.

Thank you to my husband, Phil, for sharing my love of cooking and for the many times he allowed me to take credit for a dish he created.

Thank you to my first cooking students, Alan, Jase, Willie, and Jep. Thank you for letting me be a part of your journey in life. You are the best sons any mother could ask for!

I am mostly grateful to God and my savior, Jesus Christ, for giving me the hope of living forever and the peace of mind to live in this troubled world with pure joy.

And, lastly, thank you to my friend, co-grandparent, and cowriter, Chrys Howard. Neither one of us ever dreamed we would write a cookbook together. But we do know this—God arms those He assigns to do a task. With her writing skills and my cooking skills, we were able to get the job done. Thank you, Chrys, for leading me through this experience. Now let's get back to being grandmothers to some of the best grandkids ever! 🐦

Above: *Chrys and I had a great time celebrating Bella's birthday with her. In the background you can see a tent. Thankfully Bella excused us from the overnight part of the party.*

Index

Page numbers in italics refer to illustrations.

Permissions and Acknowledgments

Duck Dynasty and the A&E logo are trademarks of A&E Television Networks, LLC.

The Duck Commander logo is a trademark of Duck Commander, Inc.

Photographs

© A&E® Television Networks, LLC: 17, 36, 84, 87, 88, 95, 106, 107, 108, 189, 192, 195

© Photography by Jennifer Davick: 9, 14, 18, 31, 34, 39, 51, 54, 58, 71, 74, 79, 93, 98, 100, 113, 117, 120, 137, 141, 144, 157, 158, 162, 175, 176, 181, 198, 203, 207, 219, 223, 226

© Photography by Russell A. Graves: vii, x, xiii, xviii, 4, 6, 13, 20, 27, 40, 44, 60, 64, 80, 102, 146, 166, 170, 184

Courtesy of Chrys Howard: 85, 124, 131, 150, 153, 194, 212, 221

© Hunt Studio: ii

Courtesy of the Robertson Family: 5, 7, 24, 25, 26, 45, 46, 47, 65, 66, 72, 77, 108, 128, 129, 130, 151, 152, 171, 172, 173, 193, 209, 213, 214, 229

MORE BOOKS FROM YOUR
DUCK DYNASTY FAVORITES!

Available wherever books are sold or at SimonandSchuster.com

HOWARD BOOKS
A Division of Simon & Schuster
A CBS COMPANY